SHORT CUTS

INTRODUCTIONS TO FILM STUDIES

D1235298

OTHER TITLES IN THE SHORT CUTS SERIES

EARLY SOVIET CINEMA

INNOVATION, IDEOLOGY AND PROPAGANDA

DAVID GILLESPIE

WALLFLOWER

LONDON

CONTENTS

LIST OF ILLUSTRATIONS

ACKNOWLEDGEMENTS

I would like to thank the following for their help: Frank Beardow of the University of Sunderland, Julian Graffy of the School of Slavonic and East European Studies, and Graham Roberts of the University of Surrey. I would also like to thank the British Film Institute for the provision of stills, and, most importantly, Natasha, for patiently sitting through seemingly endless viewings of these films and her continual support throughout this project.

This book is intended to help all students of Soviet cinema through an examination of the major works by the directors of what has come to be known as the 'golden age' of Soviet cinema. Between the years of 1924 and 1930 Soviet directors produced a number of films which are still proclaimed as among the most influential in world cinema. Even today, when the Soviet Union is no more, the interest in these films and the people who made them is immense. I hope that this book will help to illuminate the significance of their work to a contemporary reader.

I intend to examine in detail key films of the period primarily from an aesthetic point of view. Whereas it would be impossible to separate Soviet cinema of these years from its historical or socio-political context, it is clearly not enough to view film as simply a reflection of these times, a visual illustration of the ideological dynamics of the 1920s. I have also kept abstract theoretical discussion to a minimum, so as to concentrate on the films as texts.

My choice of directors is deliberate, although some may ask why there is no separate chapter devoted to, say, Grigory Kozintsev and Leonid Trauberg, Boris Barnet or Fridrikh Ermler. Barnet and Ermler (as well as Iakov Protazanov) have been admirably dealt with in Denise Youngblood's *Movies for the Masses: Popular Cinema and Soviet Society in the 1920s* (1992), and with the exception of a few films from this period that are discussed here in detail, Kozintsev and Trauberg are better known for their subsequent films (especially in the 1930s). Rather, I hope to present the contribution of Kuleshov, Eisenstein, Pudovkin, Vertov and Dovzhenko to cinematic art in general, and in particular to Soviet cinema in its formative years.

I have also chosen to look briefly at some films from later decades (for example those by Eisenstein, Pudovkin and Dovzhenko) in order to illustrate how some directors fared under a much more restrictive censorship, and to show how Soviet cinema fundamentally changed after its 'golden age'.

This is not a study of the Soviet cinema industry – that has already been done superbly by Peter Kenez in his *Cinema and Soviet Society, 1917–1953* (1992). Here, I aim to examine some key films of the period in terms fully accessible to the student of Russian and European cinema.

I have adopted the American Library of Congress transliteration for Cyrillic names and titles, apart from many well-known names. Certain Christian names have been anglicised, and names ending in -ii have been modified to -y. The spelling 'ks' in names has been rendered as the more recognisable 'x'. In transliteration, the ' usually used to indicate a Russian soft sign has been omitted for greater clarity of the Romanised word.

INTRODUCTION: THE GOLDEN AGE OF SOVIET CINEMA

The 'golden age' of Soviet cinema is generally regarded to be the years from 1924, when Lev Kuleshov's film *The Extraordinary Adventures of Mr West in the Land of the Bolsheviks* was released, until 1930 and the last great Soviet silent film, Alexander Dovzhenko's *Earth*. During these years several young Soviet directors, inspired by the 'clean sweep' of the 1917 October Revolution, advanced the theory and practice of what was still a young art form and at the same time made an immeasurable contribution to film art as a whole. Not only did film become the dominant form of entertainment for the urban masses in Soviet Russia in these years, but the reputations of its major practitioners were established for posterity. The golden age came to an end at the beginning of the 1930s, due primarily to two quite different reasons: the coming of sound, and the Communist Party's increasing control and regimentation of all forms of art. It is therefore significant that of all the major directors – Lev Kuleshov, Dziga Vertov, Vsevolod Pudovkin, Sergei Eisenstein, Iakov Protazanov and Alexander Dovzhenko – only Eisenstein (and, to a much lesser extent, Protazanov) made important sound films that would both bear the marks of their individuality and be remembered in subsequent years.

Because all forms of Soviet art are closely connected with the events of the day, especially in the years immediately following the Revolution, some historical and political background is necessary. In February 1917 Tsar Nicholas II abdicated in the face of mounting public discontent over the conduct of a disastrous war, and was replaced by a Provisional Government eventually headed by Alexander Kerensky. Kerensky's Government, however, had precious little popular support, largely because it continued Russia's commitment to the First World War. In April that same year, Lenin arrived in St Petersburg's Finland Station from his Swiss exile (in a sealed train funded by the German Government), and by July was a wanted man and on the run. He called for opposition to the Provisional Government and an immediate exit from the war. Following an abortive coup in August by General Kornilov, the Provisional Government lost its few remaining supporters among the military and liberal politicians. Isolated and abandoned by virtually everyone, it was easily removed from office when the Bolsheviks occupied the Winter Palace in October (November according to the new calendar adopted shortly afterwards). The October Revolution, then, was essentially a Bolshevik *coup d'état* effected in the capital, St Petersburg, by a relatively small group of determined but organised political opportunists, led by Vladimir Lenin, whose abiding genius lay in his ability to see that at a particular moment power was there for the taking, and that history could be changed forever.

It is one thing to seize power, and quite another to hold on to it. The democratically elected Constituent Assembly was forcibly dispersed by the Bolsheviks in January 1918, as they established their own 'dictatorship of the proletariat' through workers' councils, known as soviets, dominated and controlled by the Bolsheviks. As opposition to Lenin and the Bolsheviks hardened, especially in the military, Civil War broke out. The struggle for Russia became concentrated in the battle between Reds (Bolsheviks and their supporters) and Whites (a coalition of all anti-Bolshevik forces, a broad spectrum from liberal democrats to die-hard monarchists). In July 1918 the Tsar and all of his family, who had been placed under arrest by the Provisional Government, were executed by the Bolsheviks.

Civil War raged for more than two years, but by 1920 the White forces, who had been aided by foreign interventionist troops from, among others, France, Britain and the USA, had been largely defeated and ejected from

Russia. The country was by now largely devastated and in 1921 Lenin inaugurated the New Economic Policy (NEP), which was intended to revive the economy after the forced requisitions and nationalisation of War Communism. A certain amount of private enterprise was allowed in the economy, especially in the service and food sectors.

Lenin died in 1924, and Joseph Stalin became General Secretary of the Communist Party. Stalin's main rival for power was the charismatic and forceful Leon Trotsky who, as the man who had founded the Red Army, was largely credited with winning the Civil War. By 1929 Stalin was victorious, Trotsky was expelled from the Party and exiled abroad. It was also in this year that the NEP was effectively over as Stalin introduced the first of his Five-Year plans to industrialise the country. The Five-Year Plans were implemented at the same time as agriculture was collectivised, as individual holdings were abolished and the peasants organised into large collectives under the direct supervision of a Party representative.[1]

These were tumultuous years, and the ferment found expression in all areas of the arts. Throughout the 1920s the Party made various pronouncements on how the arts should support socialist construction, but in the late 1920s the atmosphere was more militant. Several groupings claimed to speak for the Party and to be its agent, as a result of which there was widespread enmity and tension. The Party took matters into its own hands in 1932 by banning all cultural organisations and uniting artists into professional unions, all under Party control. Socialist realism, a rather vague term that had been discussed in the periodical press for several years, became official cultural policy in 1934, the 'basic method' of all artistic creativity. The period of Soviet cultural experiment was over, and with it the golden age of the cinema.

A particular feature of Soviet cinema in the 1920s is the youth of the directors, and this is not fortuitous. Only Protazanov had an established reputation in the pre-Revolutionary period, and he emigrated during the Civil War to Germany and France, returning to the Soviet Union in 1923. Most of the actors and directors in Russian films before 1917, such as the star of Russian movies Ivan Mozzhukhin (subsequently known in France as 'Mosjoukine'), left Russia in the months following the Bolsheviks' seizure of power. Others, such as the prolific director Evgeny Bauer and the first Russian female star, Vera Kholodnaia, died prematurely (in 1917 and 1919 respectively), and before they were able to contribute to Soviet cinema. So it is fair to say that although there was a vibrant Russian film culture before the Revolution, the Soviet cinema that was born in the wake of the Revolution and Civil War was very different and, to all intents and purposes, new.

The cinema had come to Russia in 1896, six months after the first moving picture was shown by the Lumière brothers in Paris. In that year the first film was shot in Russia – the coronation of Tsar Nicholas II – but for the next decade the French retained a monopoly of distribution and exhibition of films in Russia. In 1904 and 1905 Pathé and Gaumont set up offices in Russia, and only in 1906 did Alexander Khanzhonkov set up the first Russian film company. In 1907 the first Russian film studio was set up by Alexander Drankov, which began making films about Russian subjects, such as *Stenka Razin* ('Stenka Razin') in 1908. By the outbreak of the First World War, however, the majority of films viewed in Russia were foreign imports, and it was only because of the war, and the resulting shortages of imported films and foreign investment, that the Russian cinema industry could be firmly established.[2]

Although the Bolsheviks apparently had no intention of nationalising the industry outright, this was done piecemeal, and in August 1919 Lenin signed the official nationalisation decree. By that time the Civil War was raging across the length and breadth of the Russian Empire, and film was increasingly seen as an effective propaganda tool to mobilise certain ideologies. Thus was born the *agitka*, a short film with an explicit propagandistic purpose, which would seek to educate the largely illiterate masses in the ostensible truth of the Bolshevik cause. These films would be taken around the countryside by specially prepared trains, the *agitpoezd*. Since this was the first time that most people in outlying areas had seen moving visual images, the effect, especially amongst children, was considerable. Although few of these films have survived, it is fair to say that their lasting significance lies in the fact that it was on the *agitki* that Pudovkin, Eisenstein, Kuleshov and Vertov, as well as the future directors Leonid Trauberg and Grigory Kozintsev, and Eduard Tissé, Eisenstein's future cameraman, cut their cinematic teeth. As Jay Leyda (1973: 151) notes:

> For the several professional film-men ... the *agitka* was a political kindergarten. For the others – those film-makers who were given their first creative responsibilities by the revolution – the *agitka* was a technological kindergarten. Kuleshov had remarked that in making *On the Red Front*, the actors regarded their work rather as students preparing an examination performance. Results were not uppermost in the crew's thoughts, but the finished film must have done its job, for Kuleshov was told that Lenin saw the film twice, and had praised it.

It is therefore no exaggeration to say that Soviet cinema was born in the Civil War. Moreover, the experience of filming and editing in often difficult circumstances in order to convey a message to a mass audience was crucial in the development of these directors' individual styles and techniques. Richard Taylor (1979: 63) comments:

> Without the challenge of the Civil War it is unlikely that the Soviet cinema would have developed the forceful, distinctive and revolutionary visual style of the 1920s, and without that style the effectiveness of the cinema in transmitting the Bolshevik world-view both within and beyond the frontiers of the USSR would have been severely restricted.

So, by the early 1920s there was a whole new generation of Soviet directors: in 1922 Eisenstein was aged twenty-four, Kuleshov twenty-three, Vertov twenty-six, Dovzhenko twenty-eight, and Pudovkin twenty-nine; Protazanov, who was in emigration at the time, was the grand old man at forty-one. They were committed to the new art form, and all, with the exception of Protazanov, had an experience of the cinema that had been shaped by the harsh but challenging conditions of Civil War. Furthermore,

5

they were interested in experiment and innovation, inspired and encouraged by the construction of a new world by the victorious Bolsheviks. They were committed to the idea of cinema as *the* art form of this new world, as the means of aesthetic expression of the realities of that world and of communicating change and progress to the masses.

These directors were also committed to developing an art form distinct from that currently practised in Hollywood, and that which had prevailed in Russia before the Revolution. Most directors saw film not as an entertainment medium, but primarily as a specific means of channelling ideas and images to the viewer: an instrument of propaganda. The desire for change and a new cinematic art lay behind the idea of montage, soon to be a standard device in the 1920s. Soviet film-makers also initially organised themselves in collectives, cocking a snoot at the Hollywood star system. Thus, Kuleshov gathered around him Pudovkin, Boris Barnet, Vladimir Fogel and others; Eisenstein worked with Eduard Tissé and Grigory Alexandrov; in Petrograd (soon to be renamed Leningrad) the Factory of the Eccentric Actor (known under the acronym FEKS) was established in 1921, with Kozintsev, Trauberg, Sergei Iutkevich and others all collaborating.

It should not be forgotten that in the Soviet Union in the 1920s there was a great diversity of endeavour in all fields of culture, none more so than in art and literature. Various groups vied with each other for the ear of the Communist Party, which largely kept out of cultural polemics at this time, and for the right to express the Bolsheviks' message to the people. Thus the Futurists, led by Vladimir Maiakovsky, turned away from the classical heritage and espoused modernity, the machine age and the city of the future in their art and poetry. Maiakovsky's poetry was innovative and intense, with much use of both stylistic and thematic hyperbole, and as early as 1913 he had announced that the theatre was doomed and it would be replaced by the cinema, 'the application of the machine in the field of art' (see Taylor and Christie 1994: 34). Maiakovsky was the author of the first Soviet play, *Mystery-Bouffe* ('Misteriia-buff'), which had been produced in 1918 and which shows the victory of socialism spreading across the world. In the early 1920s he also worked as an artist producing political posters and got to know Sergei Eisenstein. He had even acted in a 1918 film *The Young Lady and the Hooligan* ('Baryshnia i khuligan'), for which he had also written the screenplay.

Artists of both pen and brush were concerned with depicting the new world, and experimenting with new ways of seeing and interpreting that world. Isaak Babel and Iury Olesha were among the most original of Soviet writers of the 1920s, and both worked as screenwriters in the late 1920s. The playwright Nikolai Erdman increasingly turned to screen writing, beginning in 1927, then working in the 1930s with Grigory Alexandrov on his celebrated musical comedies. Erdman died in 1970, and had continued to work on screenplays until the late 1960s. Even the Commissar for Enlightenment himself, Anatoly Lunacharsky, wrote screenplays in his spare time: *The Bear's Wedding* ('Medvezhia svadba') in 1925 and *Poison* ('Iad') in 1927.

Vsevolod Meierkhold was the most *avant-garde* theatre director of his day, and had embraced the Bolshevik cause by joining the Party in 1918. He and Eisenstein worked together in stage design and production, an influence that would remain visible in Eisenstein's future films. Radical literary critics such as Boris Eikhenbaum, Iury Tynianov and Viktor Shklovsky wrote many articles on the 'formal' features of film in terms that could equally be applied to the literary text. The Formalists also produced a book on the poetics of film, edited by Eikhenbaum, in 1927. Tynianov and Shklovsky also wrote screenplays. Sergei Iutkevich began his creative life as an artist before becoming involved with Eisenstein and subsequently becoming a respected director himself. Alexander Rodchenko, the *avant-garde* artist and stage designer, also worked in the cinema of the 1920s, lending his innovative ideas for sets and props to Lev Kuleshov, among others. In short, the 1920s in Russia were a period of great artistic ferment, and considerable cultural cross-fertilisation, as artists of various hues and specialisms sought to create new forms and new ways of perception and communication in their creativity.

One of the most popular topics for film directors, probably not surprisingly, became the Revolution, and the revolutionary struggle in Russia and abroad. Eisenstein's great films of the decade concentrate on these themes, as do major films by Pudovkin (*Mother* ('Mat', 1926), *The End of St Petersburg* ('Konets Sankt-Peterburga', 1927) and *The Heir of Genghiz Khan* ('Potomok Chingiz-Khana', 1928)) and Dovzhenko (*Arsenal* ('Arsenal', 1928)). We could also add here the films of Grigory Kozintsev and Leonid Trauberg (*S.V.D.: The Union of the Great Cause* ('S.V.D.: Soiuz Velikogo Dela', 1927), about the anti-Tsarist December uprising in St Petersburg in 1825, and *New Babylon* ('Novyi Vavilon', 1929), about the Paris Commune of 1871), and Esfir Shub's *The Fall of the Romanov Dynasty* ('Padenie dinastii Romanovykh', 1927).

Other films depicted the new world created by the Revolution. Eisenstein's *The General Line* ('Generalnaia linya', 1929) concerns the modernisation of agriculture in the 1920s, Dovzhenko's *Earth* ('Zemlia', 1930), about the collectivisation of agriculture, and Abram Room's *Bed and Sofa* ('Tretia Meshchanskaia', 1927), portrayed a romantic *ménage-à-trois* necessitated by the chronic housing shortage which forces two working-class men and a middle-class girl to share the same room (this film was remade and updated to post-Soviet times by Petr Todorovsky in 1998 under the original title *Ménage-à-trois* ('Liubov vtroem')). Whereas most films of the time were positive in their assessment of the new reality, Room's film stands apart, and is worthy of note, exactly because of its rather dispassionate portrayal – albeit within the medium of comedy – of an urgent social problem, and the deleterious effect it has on human behaviour. Denise Youngblood (1992: 160) comments on the film's poor critical reception:

> Critics took umbrage at the way in which these two 'worker-heroes' were portrayed – as amoral and materialistic denizens of a purely private world. That they were so portrayed by two of the best actors in Soviet cinema made these 'negative' characters all the more unforgettable and Room's crime all the more unforgiveable.[3]

This was one of Room's first films, and remains the one for which he is best remembered today, although he continued to make films into the 1970s. He died in 1976.

Another film that attacked social injustice is Esfir Shub's *The Prostitute* ('Prostitutka', 1926), which clearly demonstrates the link between social deprivation and prostitution. Through the story of Liuba, an orphan girl thrown out of her flat by her aunt and forced into prostitution during the NEP, the film is a propagandistic exercise designed to raise public consciousness and encourage the authorities to act not against the girls whose only income is through selling their bodies, but against those who exploit and make profits from them.

At the same time, orthodox Party-minded critics were upset by the fact that overtly political films were not popular with Soviet audiences who, like their counterparts the world over, wanted to see films that entertained. Critics were irked that workers appeared not to understand a film like Eisenstein's *Battleship Potemkin* ('Bronenosets Potemkin', 1925). What viewers wanted, not surprisingly, was films that contained elements of adventure, comedy, and sex. Up to the end of the 1920s, Hollywood films remained the most popular, and the biggest stars were Douglas Fairbanks and Mary Pickford. Among the most popular films in the Soviet Union in the 1920s were the Fairbanks vehicles *The Mark of Zorro* (1920), *Robin Hood* (1921) and *The Thief of Bagdad* (1924). The Soviet fascination with Mary Pickford, 'the world's sweetheart', reached its apogee in 1927 with Sergei Komarov's film *The Kiss of Mary Pickford* ('Potselui Meri Pikford'), with the emerging star Igor Ilinsky, who plays a cinema usher who is treated to a kiss from the great actress. Their fame in the Soviet Union was firmly established when they visited the country in July 1926, and were greeted like royalty by both the press and their adoring fans alike (footage shot during their visit was used in Komarov's film to give the impression that the two stars are actually taking part in it).[4]

The first really popular Soviet film was *Little Red Devils* ('Krasnye diavoliata'), made in 1923 by the Georgian Ivan Perestiani. It was also the first Soviet adventure film, following the story of a brother and sister, whose father has been murdered, through Ukraine during the Civil War, accompanied by their black American friend. The film is by turns violent and exciting, but was phenomenally popular with Soviet film-goers throughout the 1920s and beyond. Youngblood describes audience reactions to the film: '*Little Red Devils* enjoyed considerable popularity among the public as well as among critics. When [the journalist] Khersonsky saw it, he reported enthusiastic applause from the audience and loud "hurrahs!"' (1992: 77). Leyda quotes a review of the film by the Moscow-based journalist Walter Duranty in the *New York Times* of 8 December 1923, who notes that 'there is always a tremendous roar of cheering when the popular Cossack General [Budennyi] is shown on the screen' (1973: 168) and Peter Kenez asserts that the film 'continued to draw audiences for at least twenty years' (1992: 45). The inclusion of a black American boy among the heroes gives the film its clear ideological credentials, as a sign of true socialist internationalism defeating the forces of reaction, as represented by the Ukrainian nationalist Nestor Makhno. *Little Red Devils* therefore achieves that elusive synthesis of appealing action/adventure and the 'political correctness' of legitimising the Bolshevik seizure of power and victory in the Civil War. *Little Red Devils* was remade as a Soviet 'western', *The Elusive Avengers* ('Neulovimye mstiteli') in 1966, directed by Edmond Keosaian.

Perestiani made other popular films in the 1920s, such as *Suram Fortress* ('Suramskaia krepost', 1923), and *Three Lives* ('Tri zhizni', 1925). However, the undisputed master of Soviet popular cinema in the 1920s remains Iakov Protazanov (1881–1945). Protazanov is one of the most significant figures in the history of Russian and Soviet film because he made consistently popular films both before the Revolution and after, continuing well into the Stalinist period. He made his directorial debut in 1911 with *The Departure of the Great Old Man* ('Ukhod velikogo startsa'), an account of the final days of Lev Tolstoy. He made a star of Ivan Mozzhukhin in literary adaptations, such as *The Queen of Spades* ('Pikovaia dama') in 1916, based on Pushkin's short story, and *Father Sergius* ('Otets Sergii'), after the novella by Tolstoy, made in 1918. On his return to the Soviet Union, he made the first Soviet science fiction film, *Aelita* ('Aelita'), in 1924.

Almost two hours long, and with a cast of thousands, *Aelita* is a very impressive film. It contains several interconnecting storylines and themes relevant to the time. Protazanov includes massive Constructivist sets by the artist Alexander Rodchenko, and imaginative, occasionally outlandish and erotic costumes by Alexandra Exter. He also offered the first screen roles to Igor Ilinsky, Iuliia Solntseva and Nikolai Batalov, all of whom became stars following this film. Based on a 1923 novel by Alexei Tolstoy, it begins with a radio message from Mars received on earth. The scientist Los makes it his life's work to build a spaceship that can reach Mars. At the same time, various subplots unfold involving murder and bureaucratic corruption. Intriguingly, Protazanov shows that the same atmosphere of suspicion, fear and treachery exists on Mars as in NEP Russia. Eventually Los, with Gusev, a Civil War veteran and former member of Marshall Budennyi's famous Red Cavalry, and Kravtsov, the policeman, set off for Mars and encounter a civilisation whose class structure parallels that of the capitalist countries on Earth. Accordingly, they urge the slaves to revolt, and even Aelita, the Queen of Mars, joins the new order. However, at the end of the film the whole Martian adventure is shown to have been simply Los's dream. Revolution and social justice remain illusory.

The film contains several satirical swipes at bourgeois tastes and behaviour, and lampoons the former upper classes who yearn for their past opulence. But Protazanov also shows how poverty can tempt otherwise honest workers to abandon loved ones and become seduced by apparent riches. He also shows the workings of the police state, as Kravtsov (superbly played by Ilinsky) pokes his nose into everyone's business and throws his considerable weight about. *Aelita* may have been a magnificent monument to the blossoming Soviet film industry, but it was not well received by the critics. Its subversive allusions and ironic attitude to social progress were not lost on eagle-eyed ideological watchdogs. As Youngblood (1992: 110) comments:

No other film of early Soviet cinema was attacked as consistently or over so long a period as *Aelita*. From 1924 to 1928, it was a regular target for film critics and for the many social activists who felt that the film industry was not supporting Soviet interests. The movie

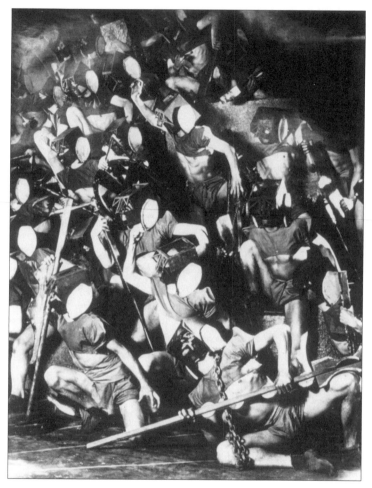

FIGURE 1 *Aelita: the face of slavery*

that the British critic Paul Rotha labelled 'extraordinary', though theatrical, was greeted quite differently in the pages of the Soviet film press, excoriated on ideological, economic, class, and national grounds.

Nevertheless, Protazanov became commercially the most successful Soviet director of the 1920s over the next six years. *His Call* ('Ego prizyv'), referring to the lately deceased Lenin and the Party's 'call' to the people for mass enrolment, was released in 1925. It was a melodrama that was well received both critically and by the public. It concerns an *émigré* who returns to Soviet Russia to reclaim the fortune he had hidden, and seduction and murder ensue. Critics approved of the clear ideological message of the debauched emigration and the correctness of Party policy. *The Tailor from Torzhok* ('Zakroishchik iz Torzhka'), also made in 1925, and *The Case of the Three Million* ('Protsess o trekh millionakh'), released a year later, did not meet with the same critical acclaim, although they were successful at the box office. Both are comedies featuring Igor Ilinsky, and both satirise the NEP preoccupation with material wealth. *The Forty-First* ('Sorok pervyi'), made in 1927, is based on a Civil War novella by Boris Lavrenev, and is set on safer ideological ground. It, too, met with great commercial success, and fared better with the critics than Protazanov's previous two films. A Red Army fighter, Mariutka, and her White prisoner are stranded on an island, learn to live together and fall in love. As a White ship approaches to rescue them, Mariutka overcomes her feelings and shoots her charge, who becomes her forty-first scalp. Its mix of Bolshevik bravado, romance and its sensational ending assured the film's success.

Although Protazanov did not achieve this degree of success with *The Man from the Restaurant* ('Chelovek iz restorana'), released in 1927, or *The White Eagle* ('Belyi orel'), made a year later, he returned to form with *Don Diego and Pelageia* ('Don Diego i Pelageia'), also released in 1928, and acclaimed as possibly the best Soviet comedy of the 1920s (see Iurenev 1964). Although it contains a social message that could be construed as being unflattering to socialist society more than a decade after the Revolution (the evils of bureaucracy, and the continuing gap between town and country), the film maintains a fine balance of satire, realism and good-natured humour.

Protazanov's last two silent films were also comedies, and were popular with audiences, if not with the critics. *Ranks and People* (Chiny i lindi) was released in 1929, and saw Protazanov return to the Russian classical literary heritage. It is based on three stories by Chekhov, all of which offer a satirical look at the old order. *The Festival of St Jorgen* ('Prazdnik sviatogo Iorgena', 1930), corresponds to the spirit of the times (the Soviet Cultural Revolution) in that it represents an attack on the Church, yet is further interesting for being a comedy. In an unnamed Western country, Igor Ilinsky and Anatoly Ktorov are two escaped convicts disguised as nuns and hiding out in a church. Ktorov is mistaken for Saint Jorgen come down to Earth, and delights in the adulation accorded him, even getting the girl (played by Mariia Strelkova). Ilinsky is engaged in a series of comic chases with policemen that are obviously influenced by Chaplin's antics. Alongside the knockabout comedy is the obligatory anti-religious satire, with Church leaders shown to be greedy and cynical, and in league with big business.

Protazanov went on to make several more films in the 1930s and 1940s, but remains best known for his silent films, especially his light-hearted comedies of the 1920s. Although he made little contribution to the theoretical debates on film raging at the time, it can be said that Protazanov initiated the Soviet film comedy as a genre, as he had an intuitive sense of what cinema audiences wanted to see. Politically vulnerable for beginning his career before 1917, he nevertheless developed and richly enhanced Soviet film as the medium of entertainment for the masses before the great ideological clampdown of the late 1920s and early 1930s.

There were, of course, other directors whose films caught the imagination of the viewing public, in particular Boris Barnet (1902–1965) and Fridrikh Ermler (1898–1967). Barnet had been born into a shop-keeping family, had taken part in the Civil War on the side of the Reds, and been chosen by Kuleshov to play the part of the cowboy Jeddy in *The Extraordinary Adventures of Mr West in the Land of the Bolsheviks*. He then turned his hand to directing, beginning with the action adventure *Miss Mend* in 1926. Although undoubtedly popular with the public, Barnet's film was criticised by the ideological critics exactly because it offered simple escapist entertainment. The plot concerns attempts by anti-Soviet forces abroad to subvert the new state, and features fights, chases and murders in the style of a Hollywood movie.

Barnet's next film was *The Girl with the Hatbox* ('Devushka s korobkoi', 1927), a romantic comedy that satirised NEP mores, and that, too, was attacked by the critics. His best film of the 1920s, however, was *The House on Trubnaia Square* ('Dom na Trubnoi'), released in 1928, one of the best comedies of the decade. It concerns a young girl who comes to Moscow from the countryside, and her various adventures before finding true love. The film also contained much social satire. It, too, was attacked by the critics, and Barnet's film career never recovered its former eminence. He made some more films in the 1930s (notably *Borderlands* ('Okraina') in 1933), and continued into the 1960s, but never to the same acclaim or importance.

Fridrikh Ermler directed four films between 1926 and 1930, and earned his reputation as a chronicler and observer of contemporary life. 'Fridrikh Ermler' was in fact a pseudonym used while working as a spy behind German lines during the First World War – he was born Vladimir Markovich Breslav, of Jewish parentage. Following service in the Soviet secret police (the *Cheka*, then the GPU as it later became), he began as an actor but gave that up to turn to directing. In 1926 his film *Katka the Apple Seller* ('Katka – Bumazhnyi Ranet') appeared, about a girl who comes to Petrograd from the countryside and gets involved with criminals. Ermler's achievement in this film was to show problems of Soviet society, such as the existence of a criminal underclass, that were actually products of NEP society and not survivors of the Tsarist era. In so doing, he risked the wrath of the critics. *The Parisian Cobbler* ('Parizhskii sapozhnik'), released in 1928, draws attention to the moral hypocrisy of Communist Youth League members, supposedly the young vanguard of the class struggle and supposedly paragons of virtue. In the same year *The House in the Snowdrifts* ('Dom v sugrobakh') was released, followed the next year by Ermler's best silent film, *Fragment of Empire* ('Oblomok imperii'). This latter film, although undoubtedly pro-Soviet, nevertheless criticises bureaucracy and materialism, aspects of life that were deemed to belong to the old world, and paints an unfavourable picture of the Soviet working class.

Both Barnet and Ermler are significant figures in the history of Soviet cinema, especially in its formative years, because they attempted to create truly Soviet films that were original and not indebted in either form or content to their pre-Revolutionary counterparts. Ermler in particular tried to make films that were entertaining, well acted and produced, with social topicality. Barnet fell into the trap of making entertaining films that were popular, but which were harshly received by the critics because they apparently lacked ideological substance. It would be tempting to say that Ermler's important and positive contribution to Soviet cinema ended with his magnificent films of the 1920s, but that would not be true. In the 1930s he also made two of the most reprehensible films of the Stalinist period: *Peasants* ('Krestiane') in 1934, an apologia for dekulakization, and *The Great Citizen* ('Velikii grazhdanin') in 1938–39, based on the life of the Soviet grandee Sergei Kirov, whose murder in 1934 served as the pretext for subsequent show trials and mass purges. Both films attempt to justify Stalin's policies of terror, public denunciation and mass murder. Ermler also made some undistinguished war films, and continued as a film-maker into the mid-1950s.

The last director, or rather directorial partnership, to be discussed here is that of Grigory Kozintsev and Leonid Trauberg. In 1922 they, together with Sergei Iutkevich and Georgy Kryzhitsky, set up FEKS in Petrograd. They were both young: Trauberg was twenty, and Kozintsev was eighteen years old at the time. Their 'eccentric' art was a rejection of the classical world of 'high' art, to be replaced with an advocacy of popular culture and the machine. In their manifesto they declaimed 'Life requires art that is hyperbolically crude, dumbfounding, nerve-wracking, openly utilitarian, mechanically exact, momentary, rapid', and famously declared that 'We prefer Charlie's arse to Eleonora Duse's hands!' (see Taylor and Christie 1994: 58–9). Their first film was *The Adventures of Oktiabrina* ('Pokhozhdeniia Oktiabriny'), released in 1924, and featuring a villainous character called Coolidge Curzonovich Poincaré, who, as a puppet of imperialism, is dressed like a clown, with chases in the manner of Hollywood films. They also made *The Overcoat* ('Shinel'), in 1926, an adaptation of Gogol's famous story which used effects such as lighting and shadow, and the actual topography of St Petersburg, to startling and sometimes frightening effect, in order to convey the gloom and hopelessness of the old world.

A typical FEKS film was *The Devil's Wheel* ('Chertovo koleso'), made in 1926. It features long sequences set in a fairground and music-hall (the culture of the street), and has a good pace to it, with rapid editing and inter-cutting used to create excitement and maximum suspense. Vania Shorin is a sailor from the legendary battleship *Avrora* who gets seduced by fairground attractions (and the girl Valia), and is late to return to his ship. He then gets involved with criminals, but they are eventually defeated in a shoot-out with police and he is restored to his place on the ship. The film therefore combines two themes then popular in the cinema: the revolutionary legacy and its hallowed status, and the problems of everyday life.

Yet aside from its topicality, *The Devil's Wheel* contains its fair share of clichés: Valia's brutal father represents the discredited patriarchalism of old, and there is an obvious visual contrast of a dissolute bar frequented by society's flotsam with a sombre workers' club. The film, however, has one classic moment: as Vania realises in the fairground that his time to return to the ship is running out, he is pictured clambering across a giant clock-face, trying to stop the hands from moving forward.

Perhaps the best film of FEKS, *New Babylon* was made in 1929. Kozintsev and Trauberg continued to direct together until 1945 (in particular, the Maxim trilogy of 1935–39), when they began to make films separately. Kozintsev in particular became a noted adapter of literary classics in later life (*Don Quixote* ('Don Kikhot', 1958), *Hamlet* ('Gamlet', 1964) and *King Lear* ('Korol Lir', 1971). Kozintsev died in 1973, Trauberg in 1990.

The influential *New Babylon* is set during the Paris Commune of 1871. The Parisian bourgeoisie revel and rejoice as war is declared on Prussia, and cheer soldiers off to battle amid a sea of raised umbrellas. The war is treated as a theatrical spectacle by the bourgeoisie, as they announce ticket prices for the show. Only the workers will suffer in this war. We are

17

introduced to the heroine Louise, the target of the theatre manager's lustful attention. 'Gay Paris' is presented in suitably lascivious and sensuous images, with drinking, dancing and furious declaiming by the assembled soaks. Throughout the film the war-theatre analogy is maintained, so that at the end, when the French army cannons fire on the Communards, the observing bourgeoisie applaud and cheer, as if watching a play or opera.

The Government and the bourgeoisie are prepared to surrender to the Prussians as the French army is defeated, but the workers organise a militia to resist foreign occupation. The quiet dignity of the workers is shown in sharp contrast to the self-indulgence of the bourgeoisie. Kozintsev and Trauberg concentrate on the faces of individuals, showing emotions and reactions which are not only individualised, but are also determined by class. Thus the bourgeoisie respond as one to a given situation, as do the workers (although the workers are more humanised). The womenfolk prevent the French army from seizing the cannons from the workers' militia, as they know that the guns will be turned against the workers by the army, in league with the Prussians and the bourgeoisie.

The workers establish the Paris Commune as the old order is swept away, represented in shots of glum statues and gargoyles, and the affirmation of a series of slogans that would not be out of place in Bolshevik terminology: 'We will work for ourselves, and not for the bosses – that is what the Commune has resolved'; 'Our children will not be the cannon fodder of the rich – that is what the Commune has resolved'; 'We will not be thrown out of our homes – that is what the Commune has resolved'. The final sentiment could have been devised by Lenin himself: 'Before us is eternity – we will succeed in resolving everything'.

The final episodes of the film see the French Government signing a peace treaty with the Prussians and then moving against the Commune. The Commune is crushed, Louise and her surviving Communards are executed, and the old order is re-established amid the familiar revelry and licentiousness. But, as the cry of 'Long Live the Commune!' goes up, we know that this is merely an interlude, that history has taken a decisive step forward and the global struggle for freedom will eventually be triumphant with the victory of the Bolsheviks in 1917.

The critical debate of 'entertainment versus education' continued throughout the 1920s, and was effectively brought to an end with the Cultural Revolution that took place in the last years of the decade. As with every other aspect of national culture, the Party took complete control of the cinema in 1928–29. Lenin is reported to have claimed it as 'the most important of all the arts' in 1922, and in 1923 Trotsky called it 'the most important weapon' in propaganda: 'this weapon which cries out to be used, is the best instrument for propaganda, technical, educational and industrial propaganda ... a propaganda which is accessible to everyone' (see Taylor and Christie 1994: 95). The Party Conference on Cinema in 1928 resolved that Soviet cinema must be guided by the correct socio-political content in accordance with the ideology of the proletariat:

Hence the socio-political content of Soviet cinema amounts to propaganda through the depiction of the new socialist elements in the economy, in social relations, in everyday life and in the personality of man; to struggle against the remnants of the old order; to the enlightenment of the masses, in their education and organisation around the cultural, economic and political tasks of the proletariat and its Party, realised in the period of socialist construction; to the class elucidation of historical events and social phenomena; to the dissemination of general knowledge and international education of the masses; to overcoming the national prejudices and provincial narrow-mindedness of the masses and giving them access through cinema to the greatest achievements of world culture; to the organisation of leisure and entertainment, but in such a way that even 'entertainment' material in cinema organises the ideas and feelings of the audience in the direction that the proletariat requires.[5]

By 1928 the Party had at last resolved to take full control of the cinema. The industry may have been nationalised in 1919, but this was in the middle of a chaotic Civil War when film stock and production facilities were severely disrupted. In 1922 Goskino was set up to oversee and organise the industry, but this, too, was a failure, largely because Goskino was given neither funds nor time. It was replaced by Sovkino in 1924, under whose auspices the film studies in Leningrad and Moscow were significantly developed. The Party Resolution in March 1928 as outlined above is a clear indication that it had decided not only to manage the industry, but to direct and control every aspect of it. The big difference with what had gone before is succinctly summarised by Taylor (1979: 157):

> In the mobilisation of the masses during the first Five-Year Plan the cinema was to play an important part. In the 1920s Soviet film-makers had been able to portray reality as they saw it; in the 1930s they had to portray reality as the Party saw it. Reality as it really was yielded to reality as it ought to be, and that new reality was called 'Socialist Realism'.

Soviet cinema emerged from the chaos of Revolution and Civil War, and the future practitioners of its golden age came from a variety of occupations: Vertov considered becoming a doctor, Kuleshov had been a theatrical designer, Eisenstein had trained as an engineer, Pudovkin could have been a scientist, Dovzhenko a schoolteacher. Furthermore, Ermler had been in the *Cheka*, the Soviet secret police, Barnet had been a professional boxer, and Room a dentist.

The new cinema of the 1930s was to be a cinema for the millions, with characters and stories that the people could understand and easily identify with, under firm Party guidance and control. This meant that the role and power of the director, the mainstay of the golden age, was to be curtailed, and the primary importance would lie in the script, after it had been approved by the Party. There would be little room for directorial individuality or flamboyance (with some outstanding exceptions) and Soviet films would remain predominantly formulaic and ideologically stereotyped until after Stalin's death. It remains an irony that, despite the decades and the hundreds of films that have come and gone since, we still recall a few years in the mid-to-late 1920s as a time when half a dozen Soviet directors showed the world what cinema could be, and thereby helped establish it as the major art form of the twentieth century.

1 LEV KULESHOV: THE ORIGINS OF MONTAGE IN SOVIET CINEMA

Lev Kuleshov is the first theorist of Soviet cinema, and as such played a more significant part in the development of the golden age than any other figure, with the possible exception of Eisenstein. It was Kuleshov who advanced the theory of montage, based on his viewing of American films (especially D. W. Griffith's *The Birth of a Nation* (1915), and *Intolerance* (1916)), and he also formulated an acting method. Directorially he is best known for introducing Hollywood's use of montage to Soviet cinema, whereby one image crosscut with another would give the impression of simultaneous or consecutive actions – known subsequently as the 'Kuleshov effect'.

Lev Vladimirovich Kuleshov was born on 13 January 1899 in Tambov. His mother was a village schoolteacher and his father, Vladimir Sergeevich Kuleshov, had trained as an artist. After the death of his father, Kuleshov and his mother moved to Moscow in 1910, and in 1915 he began studying painting. A year later, he started working as a set designer for the director Evgeny Bauer, and during the Civil War he made his own *agit* films, with his own school of actors. His directorial debut was in 1918 (aged only nineteen) with the film *Engineer Prite's Project* ('Proekt Inzhenera Praita'). This was followed by a period of frenetic activity by Kuleshov, both in the production of films and the development of his own theoretical concepts. In 1919 he made *The Unsung Song of Love* ('Pesn liubvi nedopetaia'), and in 1920 *On the Red Front* ('Na krasnom fronte'). By this time Kuleshov was already teaching at the State Film School in Moscow.

Kuleshov's best known film is *The Extraordinary Adventures of Mr West in the Land of the Bolsheviks* ('Neobychainye prikliucheniia Mistera Vesta v strane bolshevikov'), made in 1924. A year later *The Death Ray* ('Luch smerti') appeared, a relatively violent film about international espionage, and in 1926 *By the Law* ('Po zakonu') was produced, based on a Jack London story about gold prospectors in the Klondike. In 1927 Kuleshov directed *Your Lady Friend* ('Vasha znakomaia'), about a love triangle, and in 1929 *The Gay Canary* ('Veselaia kanareika'), a Civil War story set in a holiday resort.

Throughout the late 1920s Kuleshov was attacked by Party-minded critics for his explicit homage to 'Americanism' and the alleged 'formalism' of his films. Formalism was a charge directed at those artists, writers, musicians and directors who were seen as preferring form and aesthetic values over ideological content. Many could not forgive him for choosing subject matter that was not Soviet in origin, and his publicly-stated debt to Hollywood. What critics objected to was that the artistic skill and imagination of Kuleshov as a director did not produce revolutionary spectacles or hymns to Bolshevik rule, as did Eisenstein, Pudovkin and Dovzhenko, but highly original and commercially successful films. Peter Kenez (1992: 114) comments:

> None of the major artists was denounced as bitterly and as consistently as Lev V. Kuleshov. In the overheated rhetoric of the day, his name came to stand for everything that the critics disliked: 'formalism', 'apoliticism', and a 'vulgar desire to give the audiences what the audiences wanted'. The title of his film, *The Gay Canary*, became a kind of catchphrase, a shorthand for denouncing the 'enemy'.

Kuleshov's last major film was also his most ambitious. *The Great Consoler* ('Velikii uteshitel') was released in 1933, and was based on some short stories by the turn-of-the-century American writer O. Henry. Rather than make a direct literary adaptation, Kuleshov chose to use the stories to make his own points about the relationship of art to reality. Although the scenes of American life are suitably (in terms of what the Party wanted) negative, with the emphasis on the cruelty and injustice of the capitalist system, Kuleshov's film is more an attack on the falsification of reality in literature – and, by analogy, all art, including cinema – and the methods by which literature can serve the purposes of the oppressor. Such sentiments, in the conditions of cultural revolution and the harsh regimentation of culture, were both brave and dangerous, as Kenez (1992: 118) makes clear:

> *The Great Consoler* stands by itself. It was the only film made in Stalin's time in which a director expressed a strongly held and heterodox belief concerning a significant issue. Kuleshov, who had always thought of himself as a good citizen of the Soviet state but had been tirelessly and unjustly denounced as a mouthpiece for the enemy, finally made a thoroughly anti-Soviet film. Ironically, the film was so profoundly anti-Soviet that Kuleshov's critics did not even dare to admit that they understood it. It was much less harshly denounced than his earlier and innocuous films. The emperor had no clothes, but who would dare to notice it?

In 1933 Kuleshov was made Professor in the All-Union State Cinematographic Institute, and in 1944 became the Institute's full-time head, a position he was to keep until his death in March 1970. He made no further films in this period.

Kuleshov's influence on other directors of the 1920s must not be underestimated. As early as 1918 he formulated his idea of cinematic montage:

> In order to express the idea of artistic impression art has elaborated various technical methods, i.e. sounds, colours, words – hence the division of art into music, painting, theatre, etc. Each individual work of art has its own artistic method to express the idea of art. Very few film-makers (apart from the Americans) have realised that in cinema this method of expressing an artistic idea is

provided by the rhythmical succession of individual still frames or short sequences conveying movement – that is what is technically known as montage. Montage is to cinema what colour composition is to painting or a harmonic sequence of sounds is to music.[1]

An integral part of Kuleshov's poetics of the cinema was his theory of film acting, whereby the actor was merely a model player (*naturshchik*) who expressed emotions through physical gestures. In his article 'The Art of Cinema' (1918) Kuleshov asserts that 'in view of the fact that cinema must be based on a purely external (i.e. visual) artistic influence on the public the cinema artiste must learn to create the required impression not just by acting with the face but by acting with the whole body: by an expressiveness of lines'. Vance Kepley Jr. (1992: 143) adds:

> Kuleshov's machine metaphors reveal yet another debt to Constructivism, in this case to Meyerholdian biomechanics. Meyerhold had long militated that the actor should be treated as something of a malleable object, and he required that the actor 'strive for complete control over his body'. Kuleshov followed Meyerhold's model in training his actors, subjecting them to a strict regime of gymnastics and acrobatics. Kuleshov urged that each part of the actor's body be treated as an independent module which could then be organised into particular combinations with other body parts in complex poses. Movement would also be a modular system. To this end, Kuleshov required his acting students to think of bodily movements, not as a continuous process, but as a set of finite segments. He used such devices as stop-watches and metronomes to help students pattern their actions accordingly.

When the camera focuses on the actor performing some task, the audience must be convinced that the actor can authentically carry out that task, whether it be simply opening a window in a warm classroom or as a delivery man carrying bags of flour. What is important is not the acting ability, but the authenticity of the action. Whether the cinema actor had any theatrical training was also deemed unimportant, so long as he or she could perform certain actions and gestures in a manner that would convince the viewer.

Similarly, Kuleshov was the first to note that an actor's appearance was very important for the screen. If the role or even the scene called for a tall, thin actor, then there was no point in calling in a short, fat man. The visual possibilities of the medium are all taken for granted now, but in the 1920s it was the young Soviet director Kuleshov who instinctively grasped them, and used them to great effect.

If Kuleshov was quick to note the possibilities of the new medium of cinema, he also realised that the cinema required a new way of physical movement and bodily gesture, different from what was required of the theatre. In the theatre, a totality of bodily gestures is necessary; in film, the camera can concentrate on one part of the body, the face, for example. In *The Extraordinary Adventures of Mr West in the Land of the Bolsheviks* Kuleshov focuses on the faces of his performers, requiring exaggerated expressions, leers and grimaces to express emotion and communicate that feeling to the audience. In particular, Alexandra Khokhlova's lascivious, painted lips tell us much about her sensuality (and her role as prostitute), whereas her massive, frequently bared teeth suggest the predatory nature of both herself and the gang she keeps company with.

Kuleshov also believed that the art of the new world should reflect the priorities of that world, and the Bolsheviks made no secret of their plan to create an industrial society where the 'dictatorship of the proletariat' would dominate. Kepley (1992: 134) comments further:

> If the artist was to be an engineer, organising raw materials into a workable whole, the art work itself was to take on the char-acteristics of a machine – practical, efficient, utilitarian. The art work's function – and the emphasis was decidedly on the functional – was to alter public consciousness, to help prepare the Soviet population for the machine age.

The Extraordinary Adventures of Mr West in the Land of the Bolsheviks is a film that is designed both to entertain and instruct. It is meant as a satire on America, and Western attitudes towards the new Soviet state, but it is also obviously an homage to the American film. It is based on clear American models, with its chases, kidnappings and well-staged fights, and the eponymous Mr West, played by Porfiry Podobed, bears a striking resemblance to Harold Lloyd.

The allegorically-named Mr West is the president of the American YMCA, who decides to travel to the Soviet Union to see for himself what life is like there. He has read in the American media that it is dangerous and hostile territory, full of barbarians and bandits. As a precaution he takes with him a bodyguard, a cowboy called Jeddy (played by the future director Boris Barnet). Sure enough, on arrival his briefcase is stolen. Jeddy gets himself lost in wintry, snow-bound Moscow as he searches for the thief, and his subsequent adventures form the main comedy in the film. He commandeers a sledge, is chased by the police, captures a would-be enemy with his lasso and ties him to a lamppost, thinks nothing of letting loose with his six-guns, runs across roofs and negotiates his way between high buildings by crawling along a wire. These scenes are shot with great gusto, and are both funny and exciting, especially Jeddy's traversing between two high-rise buildings on a telegraph wire. Barnet displays great athletic prowess as he jumps on to a moving tram, runs up ninety-degree ladders and perches on a telegraph wire dozens of metres above street level (see Youngblood 1992: 127-8). Jeddy's Western-style adventures take place incongruously in the snow-filled streets of Moscow, and not in the usual locale of a sun-baked prairie. The shots of a Moscow long since gone, including a skyline dominated by the original Church of Christ the Saviour, give the film considerable historical and nostalgic value today.[2]

Mr West is abducted by a gang of criminals led by Zhban (played by Vsevolod Pudovkin) and his moll, the 'Countess', played by Alexandra Khokhlova (Kuleshov's common-law wife), who claim to return his briefcase. The gang assert that Mr West is being hunted by Bolshevik 'barbarians', and pretend to hide and protect him. Their plan is to try to extort dollars from the hapless and credulous American. Here the theme of pretence and deception is played out most fully. We already suspect that Mr West has been harbouring false conceptions of the reality of the Soviet Union, and these conceptions are encouraged by Zhban and his gang. Zhban says that he is an ideological ally and friend of Mr West, and the Countess pretends to be attracted to him and tries to seduce him. Zhban dreams up a false story of how he recovered the stolen briefcase, and shows the gullible American a false Moscow of slums and waste land, the apparent results of the Bolshevik policy of eradicating all vestiges of culture and civilisation. The culmination of this sham is the 'abduction' of Mr West from Zhban's clutches by a gang of Bolsheviks, and his 'trial', all orchestrated by Zhban himself. Mr West is sentenced to death, and as he and the Countess languish under guard, they are 'rescued' by Zhban, who demands thousands of dollars from Mr West as his reward.

The American is eventually saved not by Jeddy and the cowboy's new-found love Elly, but by the efforts of the Soviet police force. At the end of the film Mr West looks out on the massed ranks of 'real' Bolsheviks marching in line, a healthy, vibrant contrast to the flotsam and jetsam who had abducted him, and the film's political message is complete. With their comic names – 'Zhban' (literally a wooden jug), 'Countess', and 'Dandy' – and their caricatured appearance (especially the ungainly grimacing of 'One-Eye'), the would-be extortionists represent a social order and way of life that has become obsolete. Their attempted kidnapping of Mr West constitutes the last attempt of the old world to get its revenge on the new.

Zhban and his gang are also shown with more than a hint of depraved sexuality. The Countess is their prostitute, and at one stage is shown writhing in feigned pleasure as she is tied up. Her attempted seduction of Mr West is depicted with the camera focusing on the repeated crossing and uncrossing of her legs, and the American's tormented gaze on her breasts. Zhban's gang members observe the seduction through holes on the door, although their debased homosexuality is alluded to in their 'gang rape' of Mr West when he tries to escape. Their physical oddities are shown in sharp contrast to the healthy masculinity of the policemen who rescue Mr West.

The new world belongs to the dynamic forces that Mr West sees before him in the final reel, culminating in a parade of thousands of soldiers on Red Square. Mr West is shown the real Moscow by the policeman who rescues him, including the University and the Bolshoi Theatre that Zhban had asserted were destroyed. He then rushes off to the telegraph office to instruct his secretary to hang up a picture of Lenin in his office. The film's final shot is of Mr West's eyes, happy and smiling, finally opened to the new reality of the Soviet Union.

The film also displays much stylistic exuberance, showing Kuleshov's awareness of how to appeal to an audience using the particular visual possibilities of the movie camera. He uses fade-ins and fade-outs to facilitate the shift from one scene to another, and superimposes the faces of American secretaries on to those of Soviet women to suggest Mr West's home-sickness and loneliness in this strange land. Mr West's spectacles are large and round, a perfect metaphor for his wide open eyes that are full of astonishment and apprehension (their roundness at the end of the film arguably represents the unity of Mr West's eventual perception and comprehension of the 'real' Soviet Union). Kuleshov also includes several stories-within-a-story, expanding the film's narrative framework. One embedded narrative is Elly's story of how she was saved from attackers in America by Jeddy, and another is Zhban's entirely fictitious tale of how he recovered Mr West's briefcase. The film also contains a lot of visual energy, especially in the fight scenes, which are both vicious and exciting.

The Adventures of Mr West in the Land of the Bolsheviks is a masterpiece of technique, a brilliant demonstration of the possibilities of cinema both to entertain and instruct. Obviously based on American techniques of editing, and with Hollywood-style stunts and chases, it is nevertheless ideologically sound in its portrayal of the process of political enlightenment of a previously hostile Westerner. But with its exploration of questions of reality and falseness it retains an ambivalent dimension, one which can be interpreted further to hint at a criticism of Soviet society itself. After all, is the 'real' Soviet Union Mr West is shown at the end of the film actually genuine? Just how far can we believe our eyes, when everything that Mr West has seen in the first part of the film has been shown to be false? Still, with its apparent tribute to American cinema, the film paved the way for Bolshevik-minded critics to denounce Kuleshov, and thus to hasten the creative end of the father of Soviet cinema.

Kuleshov's next film, *The Death Ray*, is patently more ideologically straightforward. In an unnamed capitalist country (presumably in Western Europe) the workers of the 'Helium' factory organise a rally which is savagely suppressed by the authorities, and its leader Thomas Lann is arrested and sentenced to death. He escapes from the police, and travels to the Soviet Union where he meets the engineer Podobed, who has developed a 'death ray' that can ignite fuel and blow up vehicles (in particular the aeroplanes the 'Helium' bosses want to use to bomb the workers' homes). At the same time a fascist cell has infiltrated the USSR, headed by Major Hart, and attempts to steal the invention to use it as a devastating weapon against the workers of the 'Helium' factory. A series of adventures, chases and fights ensues, at the end of which Lann recovers the death ray and returns to his homeland just as the workers are rising against their capitalist masters. Despite the overt political message, and its explicit support for the 'dictatorship of the proletariat', *The Death Ray* was attacked by critics for its 'Americanism', which was seen as imitative and ultimately contrived.

The Death Ray, like *Mr West*, is a standard adventure film with ideological trappings. It contains exciting stunts and chases, and some of the fighting is extremely violent and bloody, even by today's graphic standards. But it does contain an excessive amount of artifice and contrived plot development: Lann's escape from prison is ludicrously easy, with an open window beckoning, a rope invitingly draped down the prison wall to help him, and not a sign of a warder or policeman. Also, there are too many characters, as if Kuleshov merely wanted to give his regular acting stable a part, no matter how small. So, among the actors we recognise Khokhlova, Pudovkin, Komarov and Podobed from *Mr West*, as well as Vladimir Fogel, Petr Galadzhev and Leonid Obolensky. Too many characters fulfil too few roles, and the plot has too many twists to justify its essential simplicity.

The film's anti-capitalist stance is perfectly in tune with Bolshevik propaganda. The factory bosses and their fascist agents are caricatured in one-dimensional terms, with their cigar-chomping smugness, neatly tailored suits and well-groomed whiskers. They force their workers to endure extra hours when they receive a huge order for weapons for Venezuela (presumably to be used against the local workers and peasants), and their villainy reaches its apogee when the factory director Ruller is poisoned by his own nephew, who only wants to inherit the old man's wealth.

The Death Ray contains characteristic directorial flourishes, such as constant close-ups of faces that convey the whole range of emotions (especially Khokhlova's astonishingly expressive features and mouth) through grimaces, a half-turn of the head, and especially wide-open eyes. Actors' movements are dynamic, and Kuleshov again includes several embedded narratives as characters relate events from the past, which the viewer sees enacted.

Despite on-going problems with the critics, Kuleshov continued to use the American models for his films, and *By the Law* is based on a story by Jack London ('The Unexpected', written in 1907). It is set on the Yukon during the gold rush (but actually filmed, very convincingly, on the Moskva River), and initially focuses on individuals enmeshed in greed bordering on obsession. An Irish prospector, Michael Dennin (Vladimir Fogel), kills two of his companions (Porfiry Podobed and Petr Galadzhev) in order to keep all the gold they have mined together for himself. He is restrained by his fellow prospectors, the married couple Edith and Hans Nilsen (played by Khokhlova and Komarov). They keep Michael tied up in a hut through the winter months, until they can hand him over to the authorities in the Spring. The bulk of the film examines the subtly changing relationships of these three people, and our perception of them, as they are forced to live together in a tense, claustrophobic situation for months on end.

If *Mr West* was a straightforward knockabout comedy, and *The Death Ray* an adventure story, then *By the Law* is a tense psychological drama with little external action beyond the initial killings. It is obviously influenced by contemporary Hollywood models such as Chaplin's *The Gold Rush* (1925) and Erich von Stroheim's *Greed* (1923), both of which Kuleshov knew. The director concentrates on the bodily gestures and

FIGURE 2 *By the Law: the not-so-eternal triangle*

facial expressions of Edith and Hans as they take turns to watch over Michael, both day and night. Khokhlova's Edith in particular is nervous and tense, following Michael's movements with a jerky, frightened reaction of her own. When Hans shaves Michael, we know that he is tempted to use the razor to slash the murderer's throat. Hans is in favour of executing Michael, but is stopped by Edith who insists that Michael be tried and judged 'by the law'. When Edith and Hans eventually decide to execute Michael, both can barely control their emotions.

By the Law is a masterpiece of the psychological thriller. The scene where Michael kills both Dutchy and Harkey is realistically violent, but with the director's tell-tale stylistic touches: as Dutchy falls on the table, food is spilled on the floor, coagulating like shed blood. The rapid editing during the ensuing fight conveys the ferocity of the violent struggle and the devastation it causes. A boiling kettle suggests the tension of seething emotions, and the wild, potentially destructive passions of people cooped up for months on end are well evoked.

Michael's frenzied, persistent efforts to free himself from the ropes binding him take place against a background of sweeping blizzards outside as Hans and Edith dispose of the two corpses, and Kuleshov conveys in convincing, almost harrowing, detail the sheer physical exertion and exhaustion of his protagonists as they watch over their murderous captive. Michael makes no secret of his intention to kill them if he gets the chance. The unease and increasing tension of the three living together is heightened when their hut is surrounded and flooded by water as the Yukon thaws. They are thus physically as well as symbolically cut off from the rest of civilisation, and their situation is made all the more precarious when water comes into the hut, making them perch together above floor-level, on one bed.

The film's ending is supremely ironic. Hans and Edith decide to try Michael according to British law, since Michael is Irish and a British subject. Beneath a portrait of Queen Victoria they become Michael's judges, jury and would-be executioners. With its pretence of legality and sham seriousness, this is another of Kuleshov's parodic court scenes, similar to that in *Mr West*. Hans and Edith hang Michael on a tree outside just as Spring has arrived and birds sing, and return to their cabin. There they sit in reflection over what they have done. During a storm that night the door swings open and Michael walks in, clutching the broken rope around his neck. He advances towards them and towards the camera, as does the vampire in F. W. Murnau's *Nosferatu* (1922). He throws them the rope with the words 'for your happiness', walks out and heads off into the rain. Edith's face registers horror, fear and then relief.

The most captivating aspect of the film is the role of Michael, performed by Fogel. He is not an out-and-out villain, for in the course of the film he is seen playing the flute, being affectionate towards his dog, and weeping when he recalls his mother back home. Rather, his violence is provoked, especially by the taunts of Dutchy and Harkey, who laugh at him as he is reduced to doing the laundry in the hut while they do the men's work of looking for gold. The insults and persistent homosexual innuendo only further enrage Michael, who was, after all, the first of them to strike gold. His revolt, indeed, can be seen as the rebellion of the worker against those who exploit his labour. In the course of the film Fogel's Michael progresses from put-upon youngster to mad avenger, then to vicious criminal sentenced to death, and eventually to sardonic observer of a dubious legality. Furthermore, Kuleshov's treatment of Michael deserves attention. He is the only character who has a past, as seen in the brief flashback of his mother, and our sympathy for him is subtly encouraged halfway through when he tells Edith and Hans that he only wanted the money to give to his mother. He even gives Edith his pocket-watch as a birthday present.

By the Law is a remarkable film, in that the director begins with what seems to be an ideological treatise on the lure of money and its destructive effects, and then switches to a psychological study of three individuals in an unbearably tense situation, before ending on both a melodramatic and highly ironic moral note. Kuleshov has also taken the original story and adapted it to include clear references to Dostoevsky, in particular *Crime and Punishment*. Kuleshov's film made enemies because it concentrated on people, not caricatures or ideological stereotypes, and explored a situation pregnant with moral and ethical issues without recourse to ideological platitudes.

Lev Kuleshov can be called the father of Soviet cinema for his theoretical innovations which inspired others, such as Eisenstein and Pudovkin, and for the realism and humanity of his films of the 1920s. He adapted Hollywood models for the Soviet cinema, and was widely criticised for doing so. In Kuleshov we have a figure that was to become typical in Soviet culture: an artist of originality and insight, whose talents and creativity would be attacked on ideological grounds by the prevailing authority. He would not be the last.

2   SERGEI EISENSTEIN: THE MYTHO-POETICS OF REVOLUTION

Sergei Eisenstein is the most celebrated Soviet film director and one of the best-known names in world cinema, renowned not only for his revolutionary use of montage, cross-cutting and editing, but also his voluminous theoretical writings. The main concern of his cinematic art is the analysis and interpretation of the course of Russian history. He completed four silent films in the 1920s and three more sound films before his death in 1948 (two if both parts of *Ivan the Terrible* are regarded as one film), and this quantitatively insubstantial legacy has spawned a huge industry of Eisenstein studies, museums, research groups and monographs.

Sergei Mikhailovich Eisenstein was born in Riga (now the capital of Latvia) in January 1898, the son of a prominent architect and civil engineer. His father Mikhail Osipovich Eisenstein was a German Jew who was assimilated in Russian society. His mother, Iuliia Ivanovna Konetskaia, came from the wealthy merchant class. It was not a happy marriage, and Iuliia left the family home in 1909; in 1912 they were divorced. When Eisenstein was still a child, his mother took him to Paris, and it is significant that the first films that made an impression on the future director were French – in particular, the serial *Fantômas* (1913–14) and *Les Misérables* (1913), which he saw in 1913. From 1908 until 1915 he attended secondary school in Riga, and then enrolled in the Institute of Civil Engineering, expecting to follow in his father's footsteps.

In February 1917 he was called up for military service and sent to the front. After the Bolshevik seizure of power in October of that year he returned to the Engineering Institute, but in 1918 joined the Red Army as Civil War raged (his father joined the Whites and eventually emigrated). In 1920 Eisenstein was demobilised and moved to Moscow, where he became involved in *Proletkult*, an organisation that, fired by revolutionary idealism, advocated the creation and development of a proletarian art culture. In the next few years Eisenstein would become immersed in the world of the theatre, working with the *avant-garde* director Vsevolod Meierkhold, and becoming acquainted with Grigory Alexandrov (with whom he would develop a significant working relationship), and the future directors Sergei Iutkevich, Grigory Kozintsev and Leonid Trauberg. He also got to know several left-wing writers, such as Vladimir Maiakovsky and Osip Brik, and in 1923 first became involved in film-making, when he made a short, *Glumov's Diary* ('Dnevnik Glumova'), and assisted Esfir Shub in her editing of the 1922 Fritz Lang film *Dr Mabuse the Gambler* for Soviet audiences. Eisenstein left behind a promising theatrical career to embrace the new and exciting medium of cinema, a medium that was promoted by the Bolsheviks as crucially important in educating the masses. Over the next few years he devoted himself to a series of films that would show the revolutionary movement in Russia, culminating in the October Revolution itself.

It is in these four silent films that the idea of revolution as socially progressive, fought for and achieved by the downtrodden masses, is most firmly displayed. These films proudly boast a clear proletarian class consciousness (although Eisenstein himself was born into the family of an architect: hardly commendable working class credentials). These films are: *Strike* ('Stachka', 1925), about a workers' revolt and its brutal suppression in pre-Revolutionary Russia; *Battleship Potemkin* ('Bronenosets Potemkin', 1926), about the mutiny of sailors from the Black Sea Fleet during the 1905 Revolution; *October* ('Oktiabr', 1927), a depiction of the Bolshevik seizure of power and victory in 1917; and *The General Line* (also known as *The Old and the New*) ('Generalnaia linya', 1929), depicting the coming of mechanisation in the Soviet Russian countryside and the struggle of 'the old' and 'the new' in agriculture. Eisenstein thus provides an ideologically impeccable narrative about the mythical status of revolution: the brutal suppression of workers' rights which shows the violence and injustice at the heart of the capitalist system; the emergence of solidarity and strength, and the beginning of revolt; the masses tearing down the old system; and finally the struggle for a better life in the post–1917 Soviet countryside.

Strike is a very powerful picture of a workers' uprising and its brutal aftermath, set in a huge engineering factory. The early part of the film shows us terrible working conditions, the total absence of any rights for the workers, and the hand-to-mouth existence of their families. We are also given a detailed picture of how the class system operates: the factory bosses report directly to the capitalist owners, who are in contact with the police and their army of spies and agents. The strike is sparked off when one of the workers is accused of theft in the workplace and, in despair and shame, hangs himself. Furious workers demand three things of the management: an eight-hour working day (six for children), a thirty per cent pay rise, and that management be courteous in their dealings with workers. These demands are rejected, and the workers walk out.

The factory bosses contact the police, who use their links with the criminal underworld to undermine the strike. The police also manage to turn one of the strike leaders against his fellow workers. A fire is started in the tenements housing the workers and their families. A girl breaks through and sounds the fire alarm, the firemen arrive and turn their hoses not on the fire, but on the workers. Mounted police then rush in and drive the people from their homes, killing some in the process. The hundreds of workers are driven into open countryside, where they are mercilessly mown down by ranks of soldiers. The final scene shows dozens of corpses strewn about the fields.

The violence employed by the police and army is shocking, and Eisenstein does not flinch from showing atrocities: a child is dropped to its death from the top of a tenement, and the final massacre is shown in full harrowing detail. But it is also highly stylised: as the workers are being shot down, Eisenstein cross-cuts to a slaughterhouse, where a bull has its throat cut, and its tongue is then pulled out through the gaping wound as blood pours out. The gushing blood is a reminder of an earlier scene when the police chief bangs his fist on the table, and ink spills out over a map of the city, creating an image of the streets running with blood. A similar visual metaphor is employed when one of the factory owners squeezes the juice out of a lemon in a clear reference to the suppression of the workers. Jay Leyda (1973: 184) comments on Eisenstein's progression from realism to metaphor in this scene:

> The concluding sequences, beginning with a street scuffle and mounting through the Cossack riders' invasion of workers' tenements, end on the image that has become the only familiar – in print – portion of *Strike*: the equation of the police massacre with the butchery of an ox in an abattoir. The force and necessity of this image can only be estimated by seeing it in context, for brutality and violence have reached a tragic point where you *have* to ascend to imagery; the 'facts' have grown so harsh that they leave you no place to go but *up*, through actuality to a kind of poetry.

In this film Eisenstein employs the full range of montage technique and visual metaphor. Crowds rush through the narrow factory gate as if passing through an egg-timer: time is running out for capitalism. The dynamism and sheer physicality of the workers is reflected in the many shots of pulsating machinery, a graphic equation of the energy and drive of both men and machines. The factory bosses, on the other hand, are caricatured as fat, cigar-chewing, sneering bores, the police spy is sly and shifty, and the criminals live a beast-like existence (literally underground, amid a city of barrels, in contrast to the real, healthy life of the workers). The criminals, portrayed as degenerate and thoroughly debased, even have animal nicknames, such as 'Bulldog', 'Fox' and 'Owl'. As if to emphasise their bestiality, Eisenstein superimposes shots of these animals on human heads as their respective characters are introduced to us.

This is above all a film about the struggle of the masses, for there are few individualised characters, and no heroes, as the struggle is a collective one, and only in the unity of the workers can there eventually be victory. This is also true of *Battleship Potemkin*, which concerns the rebellion of sailors of the *Potemkin* in protest at the rotting food they are given to eat (cue grotesque close-ups of dozens of maggots crawling about a joint of meat). The image of the festering meat is a clear symbolic representation of the decay and corruption of the existing order, buttressed, as we will see, solely by terror and violence. The mutineers are herded together on the deck, a tarpaulin is thrown over them and the marines are ordered to execute them. Their class consciousness awoken by the sailor Vakulinchuk, they refuse, and the mutiny begins. Officers are thrown overboard, but in the course of the fighting Vakulinchuk is killed, thus becoming a martyr to the revolutionary cause.

Eisenstein is at pains to show the various levels of society in accordance with Marxist-Leninist teaching. The sailors obviously represent the mass of oppressed workers, like their proletarian brothers in *Strike*. The officers, with their gentrified ways, dainty pince-nez and disdain for the sailors, represent the upper classes, aided and abetted by the Church, here symbolised by a seemingly crazed priest whose hair seems to be on fire. The priest's cross is several times inter-cut with the shot of a knife, and when it is eventually prized from his hands it thuds into the wooden deck like a weapon. The institution of the Church, too, is therefore an agent of oppression and tyranny.

Vakulinchuk's body is carried ashore to Odessa, where it is greeted by the mass of sympathetic townspeople. In a scene that would be replayed in *Ivan the Terrible*, the crowds come to the quayside in a long, snake-like procession, thousands of people ready to acknowledge their heroes. They wave and greet the ship, with its red flag that Eisenstein had painted on the reel. These citizens cover various strata of society, representing workers, teachers, bourgeois ladies and students (all of whom we will see again in the famous scene of the massacre on the Odessa Steps). The class consciousness and true internationalism of the crowd is plain to see, so that when a man cries out that the Jews are to blame and calls for a pogrom, he is roundly condemned by all around him and driven off. All are united in their support for the sailors' mutiny.

Their joyous solidarity is brutally brought to an end with the arrival of a squad of Cossacks, who proceed to shoot into the crowd, driving it down the Odessa Steps. A mother clasps her dead son and ascends the steps to appeal to the Cossacks, as everyone flees downwards. Characters whom Eisenstein has focused on in the crowd we see again: the teacher is slashed across the face (her pince-nez is smashed, intensifying the horror of the scene, but also reminding us of the pince-nez of Dr Smirnov back on the ship, through whose lens the squirming maggots were magnified), the young mother is shot in the stomach (symbolically, an attack on the womb, on children and by extension the future), and lets go of her pram. The pram, with the baby still inside, hurtles down the steps as the massacre continues with mounted Cossacks slicing up the fleeing crowds with their sabres. Eisenstein shows us the fate of several individuals, including an old woman, a legless cripple and a young boy, the latter shot and then trampled underfoot by the fleeing townspeople. As in *Strike*, the brutality of the Tsarist regime is brought into graphic, harrowing focus in the savagery shown towards children (Eisenstein returns to this motif in *Alexander Nevsky* ('Aleksandr Nevsky'), when the invading Teutonic knights throw Russian children into the flames of a giant bonfire).

The Cossacks' brutality is answered by the *Potemkin*, now under the control of the sailors. Its guns aim at the Odessa Theatre, headquarters of the Tsarist generals, and bombard it. The battleship then heads out for the safety of the open sea, pursued by the rest of its squadron, whose officers are intent on destroying it. The *Potemkin* signals to the other ships not to fire, and to show their support, and, sure enough, it is allowed safe passage through a gauntlet of sinister but silent battleships and to the freedom of the open sea.

The sequence on the Odessa Steps is perhaps the most observed and studied piece of film-making in the history of cinema. It is justly famous, and has been copied several times by subsequent film-makers (most recently by Brian De Palma in his 1987 film *The Untouchables*, where in the course of a shoot-out between gangsters and police in a railway

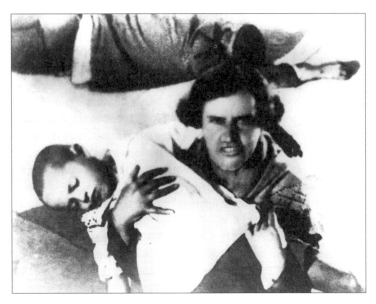

FIGURE 3 *Battleship Potemkin: mother and child appeal to the soldiers*

station, a baby's pram careers down some steps towards the rails, only to be stopped by one of the policemen who races from cover and thus puts his own life in danger). Eisenstein makes use of a tracking camera that follows the people running in panic down the steps as they are being shot, thus making the viewer part of the scene and thus identify immediately with the fleeing crowd. A camera is tied to an actor who falls to the ground, so that the viewer momentarily feels that he too has just been shot. Further identification towards the end of this scene when a Cossack slices at the camera with his sabre – significantly, the only Cossack whose face we see – so seemingly attacking the audience itself.

We never get to see the faces of the other Cossacks – they are merely faceless murderers or, in the scene when the mother of the wounded boy confronts them, ominous, giant shadows looming over her. When the pram totters then rolls down the steps, it is a synecdoche of the enormous brutality of the regime. It then becomes transformed into an unmistakable visual metaphor for the Revolution itself, amassing its own momentum as it moves relentlessly on, bearing a traditional Russian cultural symbol of the New World: a baby. The whole episode also features dynamic cross-cuts and stylistic flourishes, and there is a great visceral power to the images of violence. The massacre is answered by volleys from the *Potemkin* which hit the army headquarters, and Eisenstein shows us in quick succession the statues of three lions; one sleeping, another being roused and the third rising to pounce: another symbol, this time of the awakening of the Russian people and their readiness to defend themselves.

This episode is so vivid that viewers can be forgiven for believing it actually took place, but there is in fact no historical record of such a massacre. Itself a metonymic representation of the greater oppression in Russia as a whole at that time, it is simply a myth, a superbly crafted and edited aesthetic experience, but not a true reflection of history. It is a film that demonstrates a magnificent awareness of the possibilities of the moving image so successfully that, to the untutored, it can be taken as a factual historical record.[1] Eisenstein, however, brings to bear his own historical perspective, and one which is valid for a study of his next film, *October*.

Moreover, in *Battleship Potemkin* Eisenstein has created a homoerotic picture of revolution, where history is made by men, for a world to be run by men. At the beginning of the film the sailors – themselves 'regular figures in gay iconography', as Ronald Bergan (1997: 120) points out, lie asleep in hammocks below decks, naked to the waist and with well developed upper body musculature that the camera lingers upon. Furthermore, sailors polish machinery and in particular heavy guns, pistons pound suggestively, and the raising of the guns has a phallic quality (see Mayne 1989). Every time we see the *Potemkin*, we see its guns, pointing upwards in tribute to male potency. There is no room for women in Eisenstein's Revolutionary myth, presented to us in bravura images and with dynamic editing. At the very end of the film the battleship comes towards us, shot from below, and seems to cut the screen in two.

October has a much more explicit ideological purpose, as it was intended to mark the tenth anniversary of the Bolshevik Revolution.

Filmed almost as a documentary, but with an actor employed to play the part of Lenin, it covers events from February to October 1917. The film begins with the abdication of Tsar Nicholas II, here visually realised in a symbol of the collapse of the monarchy as a statue of his father, Alexander III, is toppled and dismantled piece by piece. A mass of rifles and scythes symbolise the union of soldiers and peasants, cold and hungry people line up for food, and members of the Provisional Government are caricatured as kow-towing to the Allies amid pictures of the horror and death of the trenches.

The film's ideology is impeccably pro-Bolshevik, and appropriately for its time, Stalinist in its revisionist depiction of key events. Thus, Trotsky is mocked and jeered by sailors, and at a meeting where he addresses the workers is symbolically obscured by pro-Bolshevik banners. The Mensheviks are portrayed as ineffectual and weak: one of them hides behind a sign 'Schoolmistress' in the Smolny Institute (the former girls' school that became the headquarters for the various revolutionary parties in 1917). Alexander Kerensky, the leader of the Provisional Government, is caricatured particularly savagely, as vainglorious (seeing himself as the next Tsar), mocked by his generals and government colleagues, and compared to a mechanical peacock in his posturing and vanity. David Bordwell (1993: 45) comments:

One of the most famous of Eisenstein's visual analogies occurs in *October*. There he inter-cuts Prime Minister Kerensky of the Provisional Government with shots of a mechanical peacock. The most obvious connection is the association of peacocks with preening. Eisenstein pictorialises a figure of speech: Kerensky is as vain as a peacock. But the sequence triggers other implications as well. The peacock is mechanical, and it enables Eisenstein to reiterate the artificial pose and gesture of the man. Like motifs elsewhere in the film, the peacock's sparkling highlights and suggestion of precious metals associate Kerensky with a static opulence due to be overturned by revolutionary energy. The whirling of the bird and the spreading of its tail coincide with

Kerensky's standing at a door that will not open, suggesting that the mechanical toy works better than the government. Moreover, the bird's spinning is edited so that it seems to control the door's swinging open; a toy becomes the mainspring of the palace. The peacock's mechanised dance also suggests an empty ritual, like Kerensky's grand march up the stairs and the flunkies' insincere greetings. In ways such as these, Eisenstein takes fairly dead and clichéd metaphors and enlivens them through contextual associations.

Kerensky sees himself as a new dictatorial Napoleon, and some quick cross-cutting compares him to a bust of the Frenchman (later in the film both he and General Kornilov are explicitly compared to Napoleon). He cuts a pathetic figure as he flees the city in the car of the American ambassador, covering up his face so as not to be recognised.

Religion is also castigated (we should recall the negative portrayal of the priest in *Battleship Potemkin*). The Church is lampooned with a series of cross-cuts of Chinese and clown masks, one more grotesque than the other (Eisenstein was to use the Chinese mask again, in the drunken dancing of the *oprichniki* in *Ivan the Terrible Part II*).

On 3 April Lenin arrives in Petrograd at the Finland Station, eagerly awaited by the masses who cheer and applaud. It is the Bolshevik masses who defend Petrograd from the anti-Bolshevik attack by General Kornilov, and it is the internationalism of the Bolsheviks that persuades Kornilov's Caucasian and Eastern 'Wild Division' to switch sides and join the cause of their 'brothers'. Symbolically, as all nationalities join common cause, the men dance together, with Russian and Caucasian folk-dancing alternating. Even in the early stages of the film, the viewer is left in no doubt about the strength of brotherhood between workers and soldiers of different nationalities, as German and Russian troops fraternise in the trenches. The Bolshevik delegates to the Military Revolutionary Committee are from all over the Russian Empire, including the East, the naval port of Kronstadt, the front-line, Ukraine and Siberia, all united in their common desire for revolutionary change.

Eisenstein's mastery of the medium is particularly evident in the crowd scenes. When Provisional Government troops shoot into a mass pro-Bolshevik demonstration, we get a sure feel of the open space of the street, and of the panic and fear as thousands disperse and flee. This violence is made all the more vivid with the director's choice of salient detail: the hair of a dead girl spread across the roadway, and a dead horse tethered to a carriage that is lowered and then dropped into the river Neva as the bridge is raised. The storming of the Winter Palace, which forms the film's climax, is a magnificently staged spectacle, as thousands pour over Palace Square and fight their way into the Palace to arrest the remaining members of the Provisional Government. Again, the emphasis is on the mass, with very few individuals highlighted. The Bolsheviks form an irresistible force amid the darkness and smoke of the square, making their way past the remaining defenders and through the various rooms and cellars of the Palace. Alexander Zholkovsky (1996: 249) alludes to the ambivalence inherent in some of the powerful images Eisenstein employs in *Strike* and *October*:

In *Strike*, there is an episode where the workers' demonstration is being suppressed with the fire brigade's hoses. The jets of water form a series of ornamental patterns that send rather mixed signals. Apparently intended to be ideologically 'for' the strikers and 'against' the firemen, the sequence betrays a stylistic fascination with the machine-like, geometric, cubist jets. Similarly, in *October*, the ideological perspective on the looting of the Winter Palace loses some of its seriousness as the viewer senses the episode to be a thinly disguised pretext for displaying, in a modernist gesture of 'thingism', the looted treasures themselves.

So superb is the spectacle that it has an undoubted documentary authenticity to it. Indeed, this scene was for many years passed off by the Soviet leadership as the authentic newsreel footage of this historical event. Yet, like the Odessa Steps sequence, it did not take place in the way that Eisenstein depicts. The Winter Palace was actually attacked, but only by a detachment of Bolshevik sailors and soldiers, about a hundred in all, who arrested the half dozen or so members of the Provisional Government still inside (Kerensky had already fled). One particularly ironic point is that more people were killed, and more damage done to the Winter Palace, during the making of Eisenstein's film than at the actual event. Again, Eisenstein wraps his mythological picture of Revolution in vivid, unforgettable images and metaphors. Another of Eisenstein's liberties with historical truth is in the defeat of General Kornilov's counter-revolution. Eisenstein suggests that Kornilov was stopped by the Bolsheviks; in fact, it was Kerensky's refusal of support against the Bolsheviks that caused him to surrender.

We can also trace the further development of Eisenstein's own personal agenda here, his homoerotic picture of revolution. The Bolsheviks are characterised as strong, athletic males, while the representatives of the old world are ineffectual, not to say effeminate – in particular the vain, preening Kerensky. A lone Bolshevik sailor is attacked by a crowd of bourgeois women, whose vicious assault with umbrellas is shown as if they are stabbing him. The sailor's shirt is ripped and he is held down in a parody of gang rape, and the camera lingers on his naked torso as he lies helpless during the onslaught. The Winter Palace is defended by a women's battalion (with more than a hint of lesbian relationships among them), begging the question: what hope is there for a regime if it is defended by women who are more concerned with looking good and longing for emotional relationships, than with the men's business of fighting? Indeed, the attack by men on the Winter Palace, defended by women who cower out of sight in a bedchamber, can be viewed as a symbolic rape of the old world by aggressively masculine Bolsheviks. They rip open soft beds with their bayonets, as the women soldiers cower in fear.

Another clear referent of the old world is the Committee for the Protection of the (February) Revolution, which consists of ineffectual old men and women. Their path to the Palace is blocked by a single strong and athletic-looking Bolshevik sailor, who seems to hold them all in the palm of one hand as he dismisses them. The Bolsheviks are generally associated with steel, guns, bayonets, ruggedness and strength, forging the new world and sweeping away the old. A field gun is shown creating itself step by step as a symbol of power and change, and there are several close-ups of bullets, shells and bayonets. As the guns of the battleship *Avrora* prepare to fire on the Winter Palace, they are also shown to rise in a definite phallic image of male potency and power.

October has more narrative tension and fewer *longueurs* than Eisenstein's previous two films, and, like *Strike* and *Battleship Potemkin*, has its fair share of visual metaphors and cross-cutting. Mention has been made of Kerensky and the mechanical peacock, and as they await their fate the members of the Provisional Government are accorded an apt simile: the camera looks to a statuette of a dog, down in the mouth and thoroughly fed up. As Socialist Revolutionaries and Mensheviks argue against an armed uprising, they are cross-cut with musicians playing harps and a balalaika, thus made to look foppish and comical. It is above all Eisenstein's picture of a mass movement, a truly popular rebellion that does away with the old order that is impressive. The general impression from the film is of dynamic movement, of time in flux, history moving headlong into a new age, symbolised by the young boy who joins the Bolshevik charge on the Winter Palace, and who is shown sitting on Tsar Nicholas II's throne in one of the last scenes. The old world of elegant architecture, sculpture and art is overthrown, and, significantly, the camera focuses in particular on a Rodin statue entitled 'Spring', a symbolic representation of renewal and rebirth.

In *October* Eisenstein has created a film of epic proportions and design, and one that was to serve a political purpose for decades in the future. We may not agree with his (and the Bolsheviks') interpretation of historical events, but we cannot deny the vivid and dynamic editing and cross-cutting, or the power of the images and metaphors with which he conveys that message.

The General Line is Eisenstein's last film of the 1920s, and the last he was to complete before *Alexander Nevsky* almost ten years later. He had actually begun filming it before *October*, but had to leave it temporarily in order to complete the monument to the Tenth Anniversary of the October Revolution. After *The General Line* he travelled abroad, together with Grigory Alexandrov, his co-writer and Eduard Tissé, his cameraman. They travelled to France and Germany, and made some short films. They then spent three years in Hollywood and Mexico, but failed to complete a picture there. Eisenstein returned to Russia in May 1932. (Eisenstein and Tissé shot material for *Qué Viva México!* but the film was not completed. Material from it was used in several subsequent films, including Sol Lesser's *Thunder over Mexico*, released in 1934.)

The General Line is set among poor peasants in the post-revolutionary countryside, and is another film in praise of Bolshevik policies, this time the mechanisation of agriculture and collectivisation. Like *Battleship Potemkin* and *October*, it takes liberties with political realities. For instance, there is no mention of the cruelties of collectivisation, such as the destruction of the kulaks as a class, nor of the resistance of many middle-ranking peasants to the prospect of losing their livestock and land.

The opening and closing scenes emphasise the unity of man and nature. *Battleship Potemkin* opened with shots of waves crashing against the sea shore, a Chekhovian device suggesting the seething human passions about to be displayed. *The General Line* opens with a series of cross-cuts of fields, sleeping peasants, livestock and rain, but this then gives way to a depiction of the grinding poverty of rural life. A household is both literally and metaphorically divided in two as a saw cuts through the wood in a brutal image of coercion and misery, as peasants are forced to sell off half of their house. A similar image towards the end of the film, showing different, happier circumstances of communal toil, will symbolise the unity of peasant life under the new collectivised system. Familiar symbols and metaphors abound: a pregnant woman heralding the onset of a new life; the coming of spring to bring renewal and rebirth; the fat exploitative kulak, very reminiscent of the factory bosses in *Strike*; the Party activist who physically resembles Lenin, and who thus legitimises the film's ideological stance. However, there is a significant shift from the earlier films in that *The General Line* features a protagonist, Marfa

Lapkina, through whom the narrative progresses. Lapkina was not a professional actress but was from the peasant class.

Lapkina's sharp features immediately identify her as a worker who has laboured in all weathers, very much an 'ordinary' person. The selection of Lapkina for this role is an example of Eisenstein's 'typage', where characterisation is suggested more by physical features than psychological portrayal. Other examples include the officers in *Battleship Potemkin*, characterised by their pince-nez and waxed moustaches, and the factory bosses in *Strike*, marked by their obesity.

The nadir of the misery of peasant life is reached as Marfa Lapkina's family has to force their only cow to work the plough, since they have no horse and the kulak she approaches refuses to lend them one, despite her bowing and scraping. The effort is too much for the cow, which collapses and dies. The scene is inter-cut with shots of an emaciated horse pulling a plough, and peasants too poor to own an animal having to pull the plough themselves. It is a heart-rending composite picture of abject misery, and Eisenstein does not let up. As peasants starve and fat kulaks live in prosperity and treat them with contempt, Marfa Lapkina addresses the peasant masses with a political appeal to make life better, supported by the *Komsomol* representative. They agree to set up a dairy co-operative to help all peasants and, although this is at first met with suspicion and indifference – not to say hostility – from the kulaks, with its machinery it is a success. Its success is filmed as a triumph of masculine power and potency, with the cream separator ejaculating over Marfa's beaming face. Its very success leads to the peasants setting up a meat co-operative, an event which sees both men and the animal world as one. In a memorable series of cross-cuts, happy pigs flee the slaughterhouse and find freedom by swimming across the river in a humorous parody of the Biblical flight of the Jews from Egypt; the legs of a bee gathering honey are juxtaposed with the moving parts of a meat processing machine; both cattle and men are at one in the natural world.

The film's ideological credentials are to the forefront. Religion is attacked in some striking shots as peasants appeal to God to bring them rain and end the summer drought. An imperious priest stands over them, totally indifferent to their suffering, and even the icon seems full of contempt for them. Eisenstein also features several close-ups of angry peasant faces, who are obviously aware that the root of their problems is standing before them in the figure of the priest. Kulaks try to sabotage the peasants' efforts to improve their lives by poisoning the one remaining cow. Their fear of the future is transposed to their animals as their horses start up and bolt when the first tractor arrives. Marfa Lapkina is now a fully politically conscious woman, determined to bring about the new order in the village. She travels to the town in order to combat bureaucratic inertia to take delivery of the tractors promised, and Eisenstein presents us with a picture of the modern urban utopia: tall, constructivist apartment blocks standing in line, and efficient transport.

The end of the film sees the triumphant merging of town and country, one of the key tenets of Bolshevik social policy and the purported aim of collectivisation. Dozens of tractors plough the land in ever increasing circles, set to conquer rural backwardness and bring to the village the benefits and security of the town. The use of this moving circle acts as a unifying motif in the film, as the director has earlier emphasised the ornamental circles on the kulak's gate, and the round mechanical model on the wall of the bureaucratic agency Marfa visits. Indeed, this image brings Eisenstein's whole silent *oeuvre* full circle, as in *Strike* there are several shots of rotating wheels and round shapes – the most vivid being the barrels in which the underclass live.

The sexual politics of the film remain blurred. Marfa is herself at the end of the film a tractor driver, a role usually reserved for the man, who is here reduced to doing the woman's work in the cart, storing the hay. She has travelled from ignorance and political naïvety to a state of total commitment to the cause, thus becoming a true embodiment of political consciousness. Such a route would become the hallmark of the 'positive hero' of Socialist Realism, soon to be the 'basic method' of Soviet culture (it became policy in 1934). The film, then, can be seen as Eisenstein's hymn to Stalin's policy of collectivisation, begun in 1928. Its ideology fully conforms to Bolshevik policy, and the director brings to bear familiar images, cross-cuts and dynamic editing techniques to show that man and nature are essentially at one. Sexual politics are never far from the surface. If, in his films about the struggle for socialism, women played an essentially negative role (the bourgeois women 'stabbing' the Bolshevik sailor with their umbrellas in *October*, the factory manager's mistress in *Strike* who encourages the police to beat up the captured strike leader), in *The General Line* they are much more positive. Marfa Lapkina, an illiterate peasant woman, is the typical positive hero who would be imposed on Soviet culture in a few years. Yet in most Soviet cinema and literature of the time the hero is a man. In spite of this convention Eisenstein chose a woman to be the strongest member of the village community, its driving force and politically most articulate member.

Furthermore, if in his previous pictures Eisenstein portrays war and revolution as fought and won by men, then here, in the countryside, the woman is dominant. All the men are either afraid of her (the kulaks) or respect and defer to her moral authority (the *Komsomol* representative, the tractor driver). She can even repair the tractor that breaks down, as she peels away successive layers of her underskirts in a tantalising striptease to provide material to bind the broken axle. Marfa demonstrates her ability to manage and dominate the machine, a symbol of male authority.

Eisenstein's depiction of revolutionary history is impeccably Marxist-Leninist in these early films. As Bordwell (1993: 40) comments:

> Eisenstein's silent films were, like those of his Left contemporaries, didactic works. Yet he saw no contradiction between creating propaganda and achieving powerful aesthetic effects. Indeed, central to his thinking was the belief that only if propaganda was artistically effective − structurally unified, perceptually arousing, emotionally vivid − would it be politically efficacious. This urge to plumb the artistic capacities of film made Eisenstein the most ambitious and innovative director of Soviet cinema.

Eisenstein created images that vividly and unforgettably conveyed the historical process as propagated by the Bosheviks. It is therefore highly ironic that he was not allowed to complete *Bezhin Meadow* ('Bezhin lug'), which on the level of plot conforms perfectly to Stalin's view of agricultural modernisation.

Bezhin Meadow was filmed between 1935 and 1937, when filming was stopped on the orders of the Party. The only copy was then destroyed in the bombing of the Mosfilm studios during the Second World War, and it exists now only as a collection of stills, reconstructed by Sergei Iutkevich and Naum Kleiman. The film tells the story of Stepa, son of a brutal kulak. Stepa is based on the actual figure of fourteen-year-old Pavlik Morozov, who denounced his own father to the authorities for hoarding grain during collectivisation. Pavlik was killed by other so-called kulaks in the village. Here Stepa is killed by his own father, who had earlier beaten his wife to death. The film, then, would be about the struggle of the old and the new in the Soviet countryside and, like *The General Line*, should have been perfectly in tune with official policy. Eisenstein's own admission was that the project itself was not 'typical' in its depiction of Soviet reality, and its portrayal of the class struggle in the countryside was not 'valid' or 'realistic'. He confessed that he was not at one with Soviet reality:

In recent years I have become self-absorbed. I have retreated into my shell. The country fulfilled its Five-Year-Plan. Industrialisation took giant steps forward. I remained in my shell ... I created the picture not out of the flesh and blood of socialist reality, but out of a tissue of associations and theoretical conceptions relating to that reality. The results are obvious.[2]

Eisenstein's contribution to film art does not end with his films, however. He is also an innovative cinema theorist, and his views evolved throughout the 1920s and 1930s, when he was teaching in the Soviet Film Academy and his theoretical writings have been widely collected and published in English.

Eisenstein developed Kuleshov's ground-breaking ideas of montage, so that in his writings and in his films of the 1920s he established different kinds of montage. For instance, rhythmic montage anticipated the arrival of sound, and conveyed images in terms of a musical beat (such as the Cossacks' regular marching down the Odessa Steps in *Battleship Potemkin*, or the increasingly frenetic dancing of the Wild Division in *October*). Tonal montage explores and develops light and shade; examples are numerous. Intellectual montage requires the viewer to link metaphors and arrive at their meaning, such as the statues of the lions in *Battleship Potemkin*, or Kerensky and the mechanical peacock in *October*. It is with intellectual montage that Eisenstein develops film art in the 1920s, for here he goes beyond the purely emotional perception of the visual image, to bring the appreciation of a film closer to that of a literary text.

In the 1930s Eisenstein gave classes on the role of the actor in the cinema, as well as the theatrical possibilities of film. He applied these ideas in his last films where, in contrast to his films of the 1920s, the individual actor becomes the dominant image and focus. He was also to develop ideas on the role of colour and music in film, the latter triumphantly realised in his collaboration with Sergei Prokofiev in *Alexander Nevsky* and *Ivan the Terrible*, and he worked hard on developing ideas to accommodate official Socialist Realism in the cinema. In short, Eisenstein's vision of cinematic art evolves into one which encompasses all the other arts.

It is worth spending some time discussing Eisenstein's later films. Although these films were made after the 'golden age', their examination of Russian history offers a distinct departure from the director's earlier treatment. In *Alexander Nevsky* and both parts of *Ivan the Terrible* Eisenstein shows not the mass, but rather explores the role of the individual in history, creating monumental images of heroic figures who fought for the creation of the Russian state, and whose lives have considerable relevance for the Russia of the 1930s–1940s. He also flies in the face of the accepted wisdom of the day, subverting Stalinist myths of historical expediency and providing Stalinist cinema's only really daring statement of individuality and truth.

In *Alexander Nevsky* and both surviving parts of *Ivan the Terrible*, both heroes are played by Nikolai Cherkasov. His Alexander Nevsky is played in traditional heroic mode, as the thirteenth-century Prince of Novgorod unites opposition to the invading Teutonic knights, and defeats them in the magnificent and rousing climactic battle on the ice of Lake Peipus. Made in 1938, the film can be read as an obvious warning against the threat of German fascism, and, indeed, was banned from Soviet screens for the duration of the Nazi-Soviet non-aggression treaty of 1939–41.

Eisenstein's Ivan the Terrible is, in the film's first part, a heroic figure who, like Stalin, succeeds in uniting the Russian people against their external and internal enemies (Tartars and Boyars respectively), and is dearly loved by the Russian people. In the second part cruelty and terror are justified by the needs of the state, as Ivan's secret police, the *oprichniki*, terrorise the Boyars throughout the land (a clear topical reference to the workings of Stalin's own secret police in the late 1930s). However, there is a crucial evolution in the presentation of Ivan. In *Part One* he is unequivocally portrayed as positive, and the viewer's sympathy is undoubtedly with him, especially when his wife is murdered. In *Part Two*, however, Ivan's megalomania and obsession with terror leads to increasing insanity, and he is surrounded by images of fire and death (especially in the ten-minute colour sequence of the dance of the *oprichniki*). This was an astonishingly courageous statement by Eisenstein, for Stalin saw himself very much in the same mould as Ivan, forced to be cruel for the sake of the country and the people. For Eisenstein to hint that the despot may be mad was tantamount to a suicide note. Stalin's displeasure with *Part Two* is well known, as is his meeting with Eisenstein and Cherkasov in February 1947, where the dictator gave an impromptu history lesson on the importance of Ivan in Russian history. (See Bergan for a detailed account of the conversation that took place, as recorded by Eisenstein in his diary (1997: 340–44).)

Ivan the Terrible Part Two was only released in 1958, with the subtitle *The Boyars Plot*. Eisenstein died on 11 February 1948, shortly after his fiftieth birthday, and Stalin died in March 1953. Eisenstein's last film remains one of the few beacons of individual bravery in an age of fear, coercion and conformity. It is a personal and artistic confrontation with the evil of the day that also places a suitable full stop on the director's own vision, as evolved over three decades, of the contours, vagaries and vicissitudes of Russian history.

Sergei Eisenstein remains one of the giants of world cinema. His writings continue to be studied for their insights into the nature and possibilities of the moving image, and his films are still both remarkable and influential. In the 1920s he placed his art at the service of his political masters, and therein lies the paradox of his legacy. To what extent can we regard him as a genius, and how can we – should we – separate the art from the propaganda?

There is just such a divergence of views among the political prisoners in Alexander Solzhenitsyn's 1962 novella 'One Day in the Life of Ivan Denisovich' ('Odin den Ivana Denisovicha'), as they eat their food in the camp canteen (1963: 70–1):

'No, my dear fellow,' Tsezar was saying in a gentle, casual way. 'If one is to be objective one must acknowledge that Eisenstein is a genius. *Ivan the Terrible*, isn't that a work of genius? The dance of the masked *oprichniki*! The scene in the cathedral!'
'Ham,' said X123 angrily, arresting his spoon before his lips. 'It's all so arty there's no art left in it. Spice and poppyseed instead of everyday bread and butter! And then that vile political idea – the justification of personal tyranny. A mockery of the memory of three generations of Russian intelligentsia.' He ate as if his lips were made of wood. The kasha would do him no good.
'But what other interpretation would have been allowed?'
'Allowed? Ugh! Then don't call him a genius! Call him an arse-licker, obeying a vile dog's order. Geniuses don't adjust their interpretations to suit the taste of tyrants!'

The jury remains out.

3   VSEVOLOD PUDOVKIN: CONFLICT AND
    STRUGGLE AS FILM ART

Vsevolod Illarionovich Pudovkin is one of the acknowledged pioneers of Socialist Realist cinema, and one who has, alongside Eisenstein, done most to promote the epic genre. His films of the 1920s contain the 'revolutionary romanticism' that would become Socialist Realism in the 1930s, as formulated and directed by Party ideologues. Pudovkin's enthusiastic espousal of revolution, and his forthright depiction of class conflict and political struggle, are key factors in the development of Soviet cinema.

Pudovkin was born on 23 February 1893 in the provincial city of Penza, the son of a peasant who worked as a travelling salesman. The family moved to Moscow when Vsevolod was four, and he was to enter Moscow University to study physics and mathematics. His studies were interrupted by the outbreak of the First World War, and in 1915 Pudovkin was called up for active service. He was wounded and taken prisoner, escaped and returned to Moscow in December 1918. He completed his university degree, worked in a laboratory until 1919 and then in 1920 studied in the State Cinema School under Lev Kuleshov (*Goskinoshkola*, later to become VGIK: the All-Union State Cinematic Institute).

During the Civil War Pudovkin made propaganda shorts such as *Hammer and Sickle* ('Serp i molot', 1921) as assistant director, and *Hunger, Hunger, Hunger* ('Golod, golod, golod', 1921), both with Eisenstein's future cameraman Eduard Tissé, and *The Fitter and the*

Chancellor ('Slesar i kantsler', 1924). From 1922 he worked with Lev Kuleshov, acting in *The Extraordinary Adventures of Mr West in the Land of the Bolsheviks* (he played Zhban the gangster) and *The Death Ray*. In 1925 he directed his first films, *The Mechanics of the Brain* ('Mekhanika golovnogo mozga') and *Chess Fever* ('Shakhmatnaia likhoriadka'). This was followed by three films now regarded as classics, and because of which Pudovkin's reputation has been established: *Mother* ('Mat', 1926), *The End of St Petersburg* ('Konets Sankt Peterburga', 1927), and *Storm over Asia*, released in the USSR as *The Heir of Genghis Khan* ('Potomok Chingiz-Khana', 1928).

With the arrival of sound, Pudovkin's career became more consistent with the demands of Party policy. Gone are the innovations with cross-cutting and the fluidity of montage and imagery. In the 1930s he made *A Simple Incident* ('Prostoi sluchai', 1932), *The Deserter* ('Dezertir', 1933), *Victory* ('Pobeda', 1938) and the historical epic *Minin and Pozharsky* ('Minin i Pozharsky', 1939). He continued with films about Russian historical heroes with *Suvorov* ('Suvorov', 1941), *Admiral Nakhimov* ('Admiral Nakhimov', 1947) and the aeronautical engineer *Zhukovsky* ('Zhukovsky', 1950). His final film was *The Return of Vasily Bortnikov* ('Vozvrashchenie Vasilya Bortnikova', 1953), an adaptation of Galina Nikolaeva's notorious novel 'Harvest' ('Zhatva', 1948) which painted a ludicrously falsified picture of post-war rural life. Pudovkin died on 30 June 1953, yet his final years were not ones to be proud of, as Peter Kenez (1992: 252) makes clear:

The moral content of most films made during the reign of Stalin was reprehensible. The directors, almost without exception, lent their talents to propagating an odious ideology. We have no recorded incidents, though it may have happened, of a director using one pretext or another to refuse an assigned topic. The talented were no different from the second-rate. Pudovkin, the maker of *Mother* and *The Heir of Genghis Khan*, played a prominent role in the anti-cosmopolitan campaign.[1]

Chess Fever was made during the International Chess Tournament held in Moscow in 1925, and the reigning world champion José Capablanca plays a small part in the film (as himself). The film is only just over thirty minutes long, but is brimming with ideas, exuberance and comedy. It also features – in small roles – most of the major figures of Soviet cinema at the time: the actors Vladimir Fogel, Anatoly Ktorov, Ivan Koval-Samborsky, Konstantin Eggert and Mikhail Zharov, the screenwriter Fedor Otsep, and the future directors Boris Barnet and Iuly Raizman, as well as Iakov Protazanov.

The unnamed hero (played by Fogel) is so engrossed in the chess championship that he ignores his girlfriend (simply known as 'the heroine', played by Anna Zemtsova). Every minute of his waking life he plays chess, even with himself. In despair, his girlfriend abandons him but, as she ruefully wanders the Moscow streets, comes across Capablanca, who persuades her of the joys of chess. She is converted, and the end of the film sees her reunited with Fogel, both of them engrossed in the course of the tournament. Pudovkin displays a sure directorial hand, giving Fogel's chess mania a comic turn, and the frivolity and levity of the subject-matter are in contrast to the weightiness of his subsequent films.[2]

Mother is based on Maxim Gorky's 1908 novel of the same name, set during the 1905 revolution and hailed as a model of Socialist Realist literature. Pudovkin pares the original novel to the bone in order to extract maximum ideological effect (it has been remade twice: in 1955 by Mark Donskoi, and in 1990 by Gleb Panfilov). Thus, there are no subplots involving intellectuals and peasant 'God-builders' offering an alternative to the Bolshevik 'truth', and the ending is deliberately tragic, so that we are left not with Gorky's vision of wasted lives and social inequality, but rather a sense of the inevitability of the Bolshevik victory and the awakening to political consciousness of the protagonist.

Pudovkin's use of montage differs substantially from Eisenstein's. Whereas the latter uses montage as a collision of images in order to produce startling and unsettling viewer responses, Pudovkin's montage is fluid and logical, presenting a picture of unity and consistency. Thus,

Mother opens with stills of the 1905 revolution followed by a quotation from Lenin, then lingering shots of the vast sky, fields and trees. The scene is set for an epic political struggle. The film's hero (played by Nikolai Batalov) is Pavel Vlasov, a factory worker. The closeness between him and his mother Pelageia (Vera Baranovskaia) is emphasised by the gaze they share that expresses not only love, but also deep mutual understanding, an understanding that will shortly translate itself into political union. Pavel's father is a petty despot at home and personifies the tyranny of an authoritarian culture. He becomes a traitor to his class when he is wooed by the bosses of the factory where he works and encouraged to inform on the political agitators. The fat, smug bosses eating and drinking their fill are contrasted sharply with the hungry, distraught workers.

Pavel is asked by a young female activist to hide some guns in his house (in the novel it is forbidden literature), and as he stashes them under the floorboards he is seen through bleary eyes by his mother, half-asleep. Pudovkin includes shots of factory chimneys and buildings similar to those in Eisenstein's *Strike*, providing a vivid impression of the space of the factory and its sheer vastness. The crowing of cocks, however, is an explicit metaphor signalling the awakening of class consciousness. A strike is called, and saboteurs are hired by the management. In the ensuing skirmishes Pavel's father, working for the management, is killed. As Pavel and his mother grieve over the body in their house, the police arrive to search for weapons. Pavel is denounced by a saboteur, but it is his own mother who shows the police, who are about to leave empty-handed, where the weapons are concealed, thinking that she will help him avoid prison or worse. All this takes place with a continual inter-cut of water dripping into a basin, signifying time running out.

As the police leave with Pavel, Pudovkin gives us one of the enduring shots of Russian silent cinema. Pelageia is left alone in the house, on the floor, staring into the camera. Her expression is one of utter desolation, having lost her husband and also now responsible for the arrest of her only son. The gaze she directs at the camera is one which expresses at first desolation and pain, then determination and the beginning of political awareness.

FIGURE 4 *Mother: a mother's misery*

Pelageia's isolation is reinforced when she is framed sitting alone in the courthouse, awaiting Pavel's trial. The trial itself is a masterclass in editing and inter-cutting. Pavel's defence counsel shows no professional concern to defend his client, and his ineffectiveness is incongruously highlighted by his sudden bout of hiccups. One of the judges doodles on a writing pad, clearly not interested in the proceedings, the outcome of which has already been decided. A guard stands impassively, but with an expression that shows his awareness of this sham. The prosecutor stands next to a picture of Tsar Nicholas II and under the imperial emblem of the two-headed eagle, thus making explicit his own alignment with the forces of reaction and a mockery of any objectivity and chance of a fair trial. A middle-class lady watches the proceedings from the public gallery through her lorgnette, an expression of disdain on her face. Pudovkin's short, incisive juxtaposition of faces and poses produces a vivid and darkly comic picture of this travesty of justice, as well as giving a cross-section of society. Pavel is sentenced to hard labour.

Baranovskaia's performance is perfectly pitched as she expresses a range of emotions, her eyes alternately expressing fear, dejection, grief and then grim determination. This determination coincides with the onset of spring outside, that beloved Russian cultural symbol of regeneration and rebirth. Children play, and water is freed from the captivity of the ice on the river. Pelageia visits Pavel in jail and passes on information from his comrades. Her political evolution is now complete.

Images from the natural world abound. Mention has been made of the fields and sky, and the frequent use of water imagery. The dreams of Pavel's fellow prisoners are also associated with nature and freedom, such as tilling the soil. A shot of a baby being breast-fed is another representation of the imminent coming of a new world.

Workers demonstrate on May Day, and attempt to free the prisoners. Troops fire on them (their commanding officer is juxtaposed with a bulldog), and shots of the people's protest are inter-cut with the breaking-up of the ice on the nearby river. Pudovkin also gives us a picture of the bourgeoisie standing by and observing with undisguised contempt and hatred (rather like the Parisian bourgeoisie in *New Babylon*), and when a young boy cheers the demonstrators he is given a sound clip across the ear.

The sense of time running out for the old regime is reinforced by the picture of prisoners walking around the prison yard in a circle, as if counting down the minutes to revolt. The guards order them back to the cells when the demonstration gets near the prison gates, but they refuse and try to escape. Dozens are killed by the massed ranks of soldiers firing on them. Pavel flees across the blocks of ice on the thawing river, the natural image a symbolic expression of his new-found freedom. He joins the demonstration which is now led by his mother carrying a red flag. The demonstration is attacked by mounted troops, and Pudovkin inter-cuts scenes of fleeing masses with falling bodies. Pavel is shot, and his mother is filmed in a heroic pose with the red flag before she too is cut down. The final scenes of the film are heavily symbolic. Clouds rush by as the ice breaks up and flows down river, and this is followed by a shot of the red flag flying in the Kremlin, signifying the ultimate victory of the workers.

Pavel and his mother are thus martyrs, and their deaths are a sacrifice for the new world.

Mother presents a picture of workers' revolt and individual heroism in line with official strictures on the artistic portrayal of the class struggle, strictures which would in a few years' time become enshrined as Socialist Realism, 'the basic artistic method' of all Soviet art. To complement and reinforce its ideological message, the film inter-cuts various images and symbols – some obvious and rather stereotypical, others inspired and provocative – and maintains a narrative tension and good pacing, largely through Pudovkin's skilful editing. If *Mother* depicts the prelude to revolution, *The End of St Petersburg*, like Eisenstein's *October*, is a celebration of the historical event and the dictatorship of the proletariat.

Pudovkin's film was, like Eisenstein's, commissioned for the tenth anniversary of the October Revolution, and it obviously covers much of the same ground in terms of theme and subject-matter. Again, Pudovkin uses his montage and editing techniques not to shock and startle, but to create a coherent and unified picture of revolution and change. The film begins with shots of the natural world, such as the fields and the sky, dwelling on the poverty and squalor of rural life. The death of a peasant woman, a mother, is symbolic of the sheer hopelessness of life for the masses under the old regime. The film then switches to St Petersburg where, after a few lingering shots of famous landmarks, we are shown the hell of factory work. The film's class consciousness is apparent from the outset, as is the antagonism between bosses and workers. Pudovkin skilfully uses montage to depict the masses. Rich and poor are contrasted starkly and vividly. The oppression of the urban workers is juxtaposed with rural poverty, and the gap between rich and poor is huge. There are particularly poignant images of children going hungry. Buyers and sellers in the St Petersburg stock exchange scurry about like rats, while the industrial proletariat is shown as energetic and physically strong, the power of the machines seemingly transferred to the men who work them. All the while shots of St Petersburg landmarks are inter-cut with images of people framed against bridges and buildings, passing clouds and water lapping on the shore, all clear indicators of time passing and history awaiting its chance.

Pudovkin's treatment of industrial unrest runs along familiar lines. Workers strike in protest at extended working hours. They are attacked by the police, and the violence employed by the authorities is graphically depicted. The treatment of the First World War follows the Bolshevik interpretation as a war of international capital against the workers (both German and Russian), and the fighting, death and misery of the trenches is convincingly and quite harrowingly shown. The film's editing is crisp and dramatic, as it switches from the front-line back to St Petersburg.

Pudovkin's revolutionary fervour is on show in his depiction of the February Revolution, seen here not so much in the abdication of the Tsar as his overthrow – although this is only mentioned, and is not actually shown. Various clocks again show time running out, and in October the workers rise, alongside the soldiers, against the bourgeoisie. The guns of the *Avrora* firing on the Winter Palace, and the attack on the Palace itself, are shown briefly, without the scale or bravado of Eisenstein's *October*. Pudovkin is less interested in the movement of historical forces as in the lives of individuals and how they are affected by the momentous events around them. Significantly, Lenin is not shown, and his name is invoked only at the end of the film. With the end of St Petersburg (the Tsarist name), we see the slogan 'Long Live the City of Lenin', as it is renamed Leningrad.

Pudovkin's film lacks the grandeur and scale of Eisenstein's, but he is at pains to create a consistent film where certain motifs recur throughout the narrative. Clouds and water obviously signify time passing and history on the move, and shots of dead bodies in water-filled trenches add to the picture of the horror and waste of the war, a war which is seen as artificially instigated in order to increase the power of capital over the dead bodies of the working classes.

Storm over Asia is Pudovkin's last film of the 'golden age', and also his least successful of the 1920s. It is set in Mongolia in 1920, among fur trappers and hunters who sell their catch to Anglo-Americans intent solely on exploiting them. These imperialists treat the locals with total contempt, and religion (Buddhism) keeps the population obedient and silent in the face of blatant profiteering. The child Dalai Lama is shown as a plaything of the imperialist powers and international capital. The 'heir' of the great military leader is Amogolan, a fur trapper turned rebel when he objects to the low price offered for his silver fox fur, wounding the American buyer Hughes in the ensuing fight. He flees the trading station and joins the Russian partisans. Pudovkin again uses montage to unite scenes of local culture, such as dances, masks and music, and to establish the idea of community and centuries-old tradition. He also integrates the grandiose landscape of mountains, forest and sky with his picture of a local community at one with nature, and whose life and ways are very much part of the natural rhythm.

Amogolan is captured by the British and sentenced to death. He is then reprieved when a document is found on him bearing witness to the fact that he is a descendant of Genghis Khan, and therefore a perfectly legitimate puppet leader for the British occupying powers. We learn that Churchill himself has approved this plan in London. However, this reprieve comes too late as Amogolan is already being led outside to be shot. In a strangely subdued and poignant scene he is shot by a very reluctant British soldier, who then recovers his body when ordered to bring him back. Amogolan is only wounded, and makes an eventual recovery. He is installed as national leader, but treated as a figure of fun and contempt by the British who cynically say that they need him as ruler in order to maintain peace, freedom and democracy in the region, whereas in actual fact they station troops and behave as an occupying force. The American Hughes arrives bearing the silver fox fur he stole from Amogolan earlier, and Amogolan seizes it. This is the beginning of Amogolan's revolt against the British.

Amogolan turns against his 'benefactors' when one of his fellow countrymen is summarily executed in front of him. He fights his way out on to the steppe, and the last time we see him he is at the head of a thousand-strong army of horsemen, leading them against the occupying enemy. He is now truly a descendant of Genghis Khan, a fearless, committed warrior who defends his land against the foreign invader and leads his men into battle.[3]

Both Amogolan and Pelageia Vlasova are thus linked as 'positive heroes', in Socialist Realist terminology. Both *Mother* and *Storm over Asia* portray the birth of political consciousness and ideological commitment to people who are initially ignorant of politics, and who are engrossed in their own essentially economic problems. They evolve into agents of change through the trials and tribulations of their own lives. Their eyes shine with the fire of commitment, their actions are determined by their sense of justice and their mission to fight for a better world. However, they remain as individuals. They make mistakes, and show human weakness.

The work of Pudovkin and Eisenstein overlaps in many areas, both in their choice of subject matter and their fascination with the creative possibilities thrown up by cinematic montage. But they differ in one major aspect – the role of the actor in film. Pudovkin is aware that to make the audience identify with the film, a central character is needed, and human feelings and emotions need to be tapped. As Richard Taylor (1979: 142) notes:

Hence the heroic characters in Pudovkin's films are individuals, whereas in Eisenstein's films they are symbols of the anonymous mass. Examples of this difference abound: one can compare the character of the son, and the tragic figure of the mother, in Pudovkin's *Mat* (Mother) with the stereotyped imagery of *Potemkin*, the characters of *Konets Sankt-Peterburga* (The End of St Petersburg) with the symbols of *Oktiabr* and the hero of *Potomok Chingiz-Khana* (The Heir of Ghengis Khan) with the heroine of *Staroe i novoe* (The Old and the New). In Pudovkin's films the characters are individuals, human beings, whereas in Eisenstein's films the heroes are mere symbols, pawns in the tide of history.

It is one of the abiding ironies of Soviet cultural history that Pudovkin, who more than any other film-maker in the 1920s anticipated the demands of Socialist Realism that would be formulated as official policy in 1934, would suffer at the hands of Stalinist critics in the 1930s for not being sufficiently ideological. His subsequent films, such as *A Simple Incident* and *The Deserter*, were criticised for 'formalism' and lack of ideological focus, and his films of the 1920s remain his most significant contribution to the development of Soviet cinema.

4   DZIGA VERTOV: LIFE 'CAUGHT UNAWARES'

The cinema of Dziga Vertov is radically different from that of the other 'greats' of early Soviet cinema. It is *avant-garde*, essentially theoretical, and eschews fiction, relying on the documentary format to create a new cinema, a new way of seeing reality, and a new interpretation of that reality. The Soviet film scholar Tamara Selezneva comments: 'Vertov's standpoint and programme were a reaction not only to the old cinematography, but to old culture in general, and first and foremost the theatre, whose methods the old cinema used' (1972: 26). Moreover, Vertov's cinema is utopian in that it is intended to create a fresh art form and an original reality from the people and images filmed.

Dziga Vertov was born Denis Arkadevich Kaufman in Bialystok, Poland, on 2 January 1896, the son of a librarian (and of Jewish parentage). His chosen pseudonym does not have a literal translation, but suggests a spinning, zigzag motion, and captures the dynamism and sheer exuberance of his film-making. His brothers Mikhail and Boris were also to work in the cinema industry: Mikhail would be Vertov's own cameraman, and Boris went to France in 1928, where he worked with Jean Vigo. Boris then moved to Hollywood in 1942, and until his death in 1980 worked as cameraman on some classic films, including Elia Kazan's *On the Waterfront* in 1954, for which he received an Academy Award, the same director's *Baby Doll* in 1956, and Sidney Lumet's *Twelve Angry Men* in 1957.

Vertov studied music in the Bialystok Conservatory from 1912 until 1915, when his family moved to Moscow. In 1914–16 he wrote poems, essays and science fiction, and for two years after that he studied medicine in St Petersburg. In 1918 he became editor of *Cinema Weekly*, a newsreel that produced twenty-nine issues between June 1918 and July 1919. Vertov was active in producing newsreels during the Civil War, filming the battle of Tsaritsyn, and in 1921–22 he produced a thirteen-reel compilation *History of the Civil War*. In 1922 he became editor of *Cinema Truth* (*Kino-Pravda*), a newsreel magazine meant to convey the Party's political message, of which twenty-three issues were produced between 1922 and 1925. He began writing his first essays on cinema in 1919, and in 1922 he set up the Cine-Eyes (*Kinoki*) group, comprising himself, his brother Mikhail and his wife and editor Elizaveta Svilova. In its manifesto 'We: A Version of a Manifesto', published in August 1922, the Cine-Eyes rejected the cinema of fiction and 'the theatre':

We are purging the Cine-Eye of its hangers-on, of music, literature and theatre, we are seeking our own rhythm, one that has not been stolen from elsewhere, and we are finding it in the movement of objects.
We invite you:
– away –
from the sweet embraces of the romance,
from the poison of the psychological novel,
from the clutches of the theatre of adultery,
with your backsides to music,
– away –
into the open, into four dimensional space (three + time), in search of our own material, metre and rhythm.
The 'psychological' prevents man from being as precise as a stop-watch and hampers his desire for kinship with the machine.[1]

The Cine-Eyes were against the cinema employing actors, scripts, sets and studios – all the artifice of film drama – and argued that the camera (the cine-eye) should get out onto the street and film ordinary people at work and leisure. This was indeed a radical interpretation of the role of film in the new Soviet society, for Vertov intended the relatively new medium to be an instrument which would show the world of ordinary Soviet people from all over the Soviet Union, to other ordinary Soviet people from all corners of the vast country.

Such a radical rejection of old forms was in tune with some of the left-wing approaches to art in the early-to-mid 1920s, especially in the camp associated with the *avant-garde* journal *LEF*. The *LEF* activists, such as Osip Brik and Sergei Tretiakov, also argued for a culture of the fact which would remove the artist's subjectivity. Thus the documentary would replace the feature film, the literature of fact would replace the literature of fiction, and the photograph would replace the painting. In 1927 Osip Brik, a close friend of Maiakovsky, declared:

We have once and for all to discard from the picture all its romanticism, all its psychological emotionality. We have to say completely openly that in a film we are prepared to arouse neither joy nor sadness, and that we want to depict the necessary facts and events.[2]

In the summer of 1923 Vertov published his manifesto of the 'revolution' he envisaged in cinema (ironically, in the same issue of *LEF* in which Eisenstein published his 'Montage of Attractions'):

The unusual flexibility of montage construction permits the introduction into the film sketch of any political, economic or other motif. And so:
FROM TODAY neither psychological nor detective dramas are needed in cinema,
FROM TODAY filmed theatrical productions are unnecessary,
FROM TODAY neither Dostoyevsky nor Nat Pinkerton will be filmed.
Everything will be included in the new definition of film newsreel.
Into the confusion of life enter with determination:

1) the *Cine-eye*, calling into question the human eye's conception of the world and presenting its own 'I see!' and

2) the *Cine-eye Editor*, who for the first time organises the minutes of life seen in *this* way.[3]

These were extravagant claims, for not only was Vertov asserting the dominance of documentary film over that of the fictional film, but also that his view of the documentary film was superior to that of other makers of non-fictional films. Vertov thus rejected the idea of a script, and attempted to film life in its natural rhythm and without embellishment, caught 'unawares'. But Vertov's rejection of cinematic artifice simply laid the way open to the development of his own 'non-fictional' artifice, as Viktor Shklovsky noted in 1925: 'The Cine-Eyes reject the actor and think that in so doing they are breaking with art, but the actual selection of moments to be filmed is itself a deliberate act. The contrast between one moment and another – montage – is realised in accordance with the unifying principle of art' (see Taylor and Christie 1994: 133).

In his films of the early 1920s Vertov may indeed claim to catch 'life unawares', but in *The Man with the Movie Camera* ('Chelovek s kinoapparatom'), released in 1929, there is more than a hint of cinematic subterfuge. It is obvious that some of the ordinary people caught on film are aware that the cameraman is there filming them, and pose and act up accordingly. It is even likely that they have been instructed to do so, like actors, by the director.

In 1924 Vertov made *Kino-Eye* ('Kinoglaz'). This was followed by *Stride, Soviet* ('Shagai, sovet') in 1926, a documentary about technology, and *The Sixth Part of the World* ('Shestaia chast mira'), also in 1926, which contained material shot all over the USSR. In 1928 he made *The Eleventh Year* ('Odinnadtsatyi'), celebrating the eleventh anniversary of the October Revolution in a film about the building of the Dneiper Dam as a symbol of the might of Soviet power and the ideological promotion of technological progress. *The Man with the Movie Camera* was made in 1928 and released the following year, and is the high point of Vertov's career.

Vertov continued to be active in making newsreels in the 1930s, but his output waned, as did his standing. In an age when even Eisenstein and

Dovzhenko were criticised for 'formalism', and found it difficult to make films, the overtly flamboyant style of Vertov, with its rejection of fictional forms, made him an increasingly isolated figure. Also, his insistence on the dominance of the director's role did not endear Vertov to the authorities – in the form of Goskino – in an age when artistic uniformity was being encouraged, and the role of the director was consciously being curtailed.

In 1931 he made *Enthusiasm* ('Entuziazm'), about the miners of the Don coal basin. This was followed by *Three Songs about Lenin* ('Tri pesni o Lenine') in 1934, which contained documentary and archival material about the life of Lenin on the tenth anniversary of his death. The film was delayed on its release, apparently because it neglected the figure of Stalin. His last films were *Lullaby* ('Kolybelnaia') in 1937, about the women of Russia and Spain, and *Three Heroines* ('Tri geroini', 1941), about the women of the armed forces. He made some documentaries during the war, and continued to make newsreels up to his death from cancer in 1954, by which time he was generally a forgotten figure.

The influential *Kino-Eye* follows the activities of the Pioneers, the organisation of children as politically active social workers, as they help out in a village and in a city. They check meat prices in the market, and encourage villagers to abandon the market and buy their meat from the village co-operative. They are politically conscious as they refuse to go to church, march in line, gaze into the glorious future, and sit below portraits of Lenin. Vertov is also at pains to identify individuals, so that we are not presented with an impersonal mass. Thus, among the activists are Latyshev and Boria. The pioneers help a poor widow to collect and thresh her wheat, and in the city they are keen agitators against the spread of tuberculosis.

Kino-Eye is also a self-conscious film, but one that is not graced with any sense of self-irony. Vertov delights in showing us the possibilities of the medium, be it a slow-motion sequence implying the balletic precision of high diving, or the multiple angles employed to shoot Tverskaia Street in Moscow – from above, and from the point of view of those inside a tram. Time and motion are reversed as a woman walks backwards from the village market to the co-operative, where the meat – which had twenty minutes previously been a bull – has its insides and its hide restored, walks out of the slaughterhouse and into a field. Similarly, the clock goes backwards as a loaf of bread transforms itself into a mound of dough, which then becomes flour, which is then transported on a cart to a mill where it turns into grain, which is taken back to the field on a train to burst forth as sheaves of rye. Then the camera focuses on the people working the fields in the sunshine, happy and smiling mothers and babies delighting in their communal labour.

Vertov presents his film as a factual narrative, and we are reminded of the literary dimension throughout the film when a hand writes and announces the end of a reel. The inter-titles describe and explain what we see on screen, animated silhouettes play out certain scenes, and the film has a linear structure. Still, certain images are used to cross-cut, such as when the close-up of the hands of a dead man give way to a close-up of the hands of his grieving widow and child. In another scene an elephant walks down a street as the scenery and buildings around it change. The film also contains motifs which recur in Vertov's later work. The camera observes a seriously ill man tended by paramedics, and ventures inside a beer hall. Vertov is obviously fascinated by the illusions of Chinese magicians, for both here and in *The Man with the Movie Camera* they enchant a crowd of children.

The Man with the Movie Camera is a much more revolutionary film on the importance of cinema, and its dominance as an art form in the new city of the future. This is made clear in the film's prologue: 'This experimental work is directed towards the creation of a truly international absolute language of cinema on the basis of its total separation from the language of the theatre and literature.' It is not just radical in its stylistic virtuosity, with its rapid, occasionally lightning-fast, cross-cutting, freeze frames, split screen and use of slow motion. Rather, the film's conceptual framework, in line with the Cine-Eyes' manifesto, is utopian.

The Man with the Movie Camera is a documentary film that follows the life of the city from sunrise, with people waking up and getting out of bed. The camera, the window on the city, follows them through the day, through work and leisure. As a house's shutters open, so do the shutters of the camera. The man with the camera dominates the city – he literally stands above it, the camera imperiously surveying everything within its range. Vlada Petric comments:

> Unlike the shots of machines, wheels and gears photographed in a more abstract fashion, the shots of the Cameraman never lose their representational configuration, thus implying that the Cameraman is an integral part of the technological environment, identified with the worker and an indispensable part of the industrial world. Overtaken by the mighty whirl of machines, the Cameraman appears free from the pressure of gravity as he floats in the factory setting, dancing and hovering with his camera as a balancing-pole. Gradually losing his earthbound identity, he becomes a truly omnipotent 'cinematic magician', participating in a celebration of the industrial world.[4]

The film is also a celebration of urban life and technology. There are many shots of machines and the industrial workplace, so that the film and the making of it are placed clearly within the context of production and the manufacturing process. Vertov delights in the movement of the city, be it of the crowds of people or the fluid motion of trams and trains. The camera, mounted on a motor car, keeps pace with another car, observing the self-conscious behaviour of its occupants. Vertov succeeds in showing the drudgery of factory work (stuffing and folding cigarette packets) as a joyous activity, and even shots of coal miners working in incredibly cramped and dark conditions are vibrant and upbeat: they are creating energy for the modern city.

But this is also a film about the making of a film, for many times the cameraman with his camera rolling is himself the object of another, unseen, camera's attention. Indeed, the life of the city is the life of cinema. The film opens in a cinema hall, with the public entering and taking their seats. Several times in the course of the film Vertov includes critical asides at fictional film, by including satirical shots of film advertisements. There are constant metaphors of seeing and awakening – the human body is the body politic where the perfect bodies of athletes are observed by the audience, and the camera lingers over their muscular forms and movements. The perfect human body becomes symbolic of the utopian state.

The life of the city is human life in general. A baby is born, a dead body is buried. A couple marry, another divorce. The camera is even there at a road accident, impassively watching as bandages are applied to the wounded man's head. A woman washing herself is inter-cut with the washing of clothes: you are what you wear. A man shaving is juxtaposed with an axe being sharpened. Metaphors and similes abound as human activity is filmed as synecdoche, viewed within the context of the greater whole. The heart of the city is the heart of human activity, as Gorky Street and Theatre Square in central Moscow throb with dynamic movement and are in constant flux.

Vertov radically re-invents the temporal and spatial concepts of film. Just as his life of the city is compressed within a day, so too is the geographical expanse of the USSR compressed within the duration of the film. He takes us from Moscow to Ukraine. Odessa and the beaches of the Black Sea are places of sensuous pleasure and relaxation. There is great cinematic dexterity in the film's editing and cross-cutting, techniques which themselves create energy, dynamism and not a little eroticism (see Horton and Brashinsky 1992: 195). The frequent shots of clocks demonstrate the passage of time and history – time moves forward, the future is made today.

The film's political ideology is correspondingly progressive. A woman aims her air rifle at a swastika in a fairground shooting booth. Religion is mocked, as a portrait of Lenin adorns the entrance to a church. No area of activity is inaccessible to the camera, and even in the smoky confines of a beer parlour the cameraman makes an appearance (literally immersed in a glass of beer). Here, too, there is life, and even the shrimps soon to be washed down with the beer dance in a brief celebration.

Vertov's film is revolutionary both in terms of its montage and rapid-fire editing, and its vision of the art of the future. *The Man with the Movie*

FIGURE 5 *The Man with the Movie Camera: man and machine*

Camera exults in the contours and shapes of the new multi-storey buildings of Moscow, celebrating the Constructivist ethic in 1920s architecture. It delights in the very vitality and diversity of life, from Moscow to Ukraine, enjoying, like the awe-struck children, the tricks and illusions of street magicians, a metaphor for the mystery and joy of childhood. Vertov's camera and editing also produce magical images: the cameraman emerging from inside a beer glass, trains that seem to rush towards and over the camera itself, trams that move simultaneously in opposite directions with the cameraman sandwiched in the tiniest of gaps between them, and the famous shot of the Bolshoi Theatre seemingly splitting in two. The city and the film are one, for both are created and viewed by the cameraman and director; both are given life by the camera, and the 'cine-eye' gives them its own interpretation.

It is instructive to compare the work of Dziga Vertov with Esfir Shub, the other major director of non-fiction films in the 1920s. Apart from *The Prostitute*, Shub made three documentary films in these years: *The Fall of* the Romanov Dynasty ('Padenie dinastii Romanovykh', 1927), *The Great Path* ('Velikii put'', 1927) and *Lev Tolstoy and the Russia of Nicholas II* ('Lev Tolstoi i Rossiia Nikolaia II', 1928), designed to present Russian history from 1897 to 1927. The crucial difference is that whereas Vertov the director edits the footage shot by his own cameraman, Shub compiles, edits and arranges already extant historical documentary footage collected from a variety of sources.

The Fall of the Romanov Dynasty is nevertheless a remarkable documentary, as Shub includes footage from several sources, from pictures of the Tsar and his ministers to King George V of England, the French Prime Minister Poincaré and Kaiser Wilhelm II. There are also scenes from across the fronts of the First World War, from the battle-ravaged and muddy plains of Europe to the deserts of Africa. The narrative is driven relentlessly forward, from 1913 and the celebration of three hundred years of the Romanov dynasty, through the First World War, before settling on 1917 as the decisive moment in Russia's history. Shub explains the Tsar's abdication and Bolshevik seizure of power in ideological terms, as an inexorable movement forward, a historical inevitability. Through her skilful montage and editing of the footage, the viewer believes that the Bolsheviks are responsible for the Tsar's abdication, and that the masses filmed on the streets support the Bolshevik victory a few months later. The final shots are of Lenin addressing the crowds, and then smiling and relaxed, so that the viewer is left knowing that all is well and the forces of good are triumphant.

Shub edits her material to achieve substantial effects of irony, such as the juxtaposition of the affluence of the pre-Revolutionary nobility and the back-breaking toil of agricultural workers. The Tsar's statue lying smashed on the ground becomes a symbol of the destruction of the monarchy. However, her approach to documentary film-making differs from that of Vertov not only in editing, but also structure. The defining feature of *The Fall of the Romanov Dynasty* is the use of inter-titles to drive the narrative forward, and explain what the screen shows. In *The Man with the Movie Camera* Vertov has little need of a written text, and leaves the film itself to tell its story.

It is no wonder, then, that Vertov's highly original and independent style was to fall out of favour in the increasingly regimented 1930s. However, this has its own irony. By claiming that the camera sees better and more than the eye, he asserts the primacy of the machine over the imperfect human form. In his effort, therefore, to show the world of the revolution and the development of the 'perfect electric man' Vertov in effect displays his Socialist Realist credentials, whereby the artist is required to show society 'in its revolutionary development'. In other words, Vertov aims to show the world not as it is, but as it should be, and will be in the society of the future.

Vertov's fall from grace, as a member of the Russian *avant-garde* in the face of an increasingly monolithic state culture, is part of the *avant-garde*'s ideological defeat in the cultural revolution of the late 1920s, a defeat which Boris Groys identifies as of great political importance:

> The real difference between the avant-garde and Socialist Realism consists ... in moving the centre of gravity from work on the basis (the technical and material organisation of society) to work on the superstructure (engineering the New Man). The shift from basis to superstructure was necessary because work on the former became the exclusive prerogative of Stalin and the Party.[5]

Vertov's eminence in Soviet film may have been short-lived, but his lasting influence on documentary film-making and what has come to be known as *cinéma vérité* has been recognised across the globe and across the decades:

> Vertov might be called the father of *cinéma vérité*, as his far-sighted theories paved the way for the emergence of a new style that would influence the entire spectrum of film-making. His primary significance lay not only in his ability to foresee technical and cinematic developments in the future, but also in his courage to manifest his ideas and direct the attention of future film-makers towards a more realistic treatment of the film aesthetic. His

theories, no doubt, conceptualised the core idea of the *cinéma
vérité* movement and greatly influenced the approach to documentary film-making.[6]

The career of Dziga Vertov is of great significance in the history of Soviet
cinema, not only for its novelty value. In the course of a few years Vertov
claimed to hold the future of film in his hands, and the sheer exuberance
of his art testifies to the confidence he had in his own vision. His best
work remains inspiring and influential to documentarists intent on
capturing the realities, hidden and extant, of everyday life.

5 ALEXANDER DOVZHENKO: UKRAINIAN NATIONALIST CINEMA

Alexander Petrovich Dovzhenko is justly known as the father of Ukrainian cinema, and his major films of the 1920s are a celebration of the Ukrainian land, its people and its history. His films are not only nationally specific, but nationalist in the sense that they promote Ukrainian national identity and culture as distinctive and different from that of its large and overwhelming neighbour, Russia. He was born on 12 September 1894 in Sosnitsa, a village near the town of Chernigov, on the River Desna and only about one hundred kilometres north of Kiev. His father Petro was an illiterate farmer who did odd jobs to make ends meet. Alexander was one of fourteen children, only two of whom (he and his sister Polina) survived into adulthood.

In his autobiography Dovzhenko says that he was in love with the natural beauty of his native land since childhood, especially the meadows around the Desna, and recalls his joy at picking mushrooms and berries. At the age of sixteen he went to train as a teacher, graduating in 1914, whereupon he taught science in Zhitomir. In 1917 he moved to Kiev and volunteered for the Red Army during the Civil War. In 1920 he joined the Communist Party, and a year later was sent to Warsaw as a diplomatic representative of the newly established Ukrainian Republic. In 1923 he was back in Ukraine, where he worked as a political cartoonist and illustrator in Kharkov.

Dovzhenko directed his first film *Love's Little Berries* ('Iagodki liubvi') in 1926. This was followed by *Zvenigora* ('Zvenigora') in 1928, an epic picture of Ukrainian history and legend mixing realism and myth, *Arsenal* ('Arsenal') in 1929 and, a year later, his most famous film *Earth* ('Zemlia'). His sound films include *Ivan* ('Ivan') in 1932, *Aerograd* ('Aerograd') in 1935, *Shchors* ('Shchors') in 1939, and *Michurin* ('Michurin') in 1949. It seems fair to say that Dovzhenko's name as a director of international repute rests with his films of the 1920s, as his later efforts were subjected to considerable political interference, and are today viewed as blatant and rather primitive examples of Socialist Realism. Indeed, *Michurin* took four years to complete, with numerous changes to the script, and has been described by Peter Kenez as 'undoubtedly his worst film': 'Admirers of Dovzhenko argue that the film had gone through so many changes that were forced on the director that the final product should not be included in his *oeuvre*' (1992: 242). *Shchors* will be discussed later in the chapter. Dovzhenko died on 25 November 1956.

In the groundbreaking *Zvenigora* we see Dovzhenko's mixture of realism and myth expressed in truly dynamic cinematic form for the first time. Zvenigora is the name of the Ukrainian steppe that is steeped in historical and folkloric significance for the Ukrainian people. The film marries the legend with the new political reality, so that the October Revolution is the culmination of Ukraine's historical fight for its freedom. The film is littered with images of the Ukrainian land, its rivers and fields, the wind gently rocking the grass and sunlight playing on the water. Allegory and fact intermingle in pictures of medieval knights and Red Army trains, and in the figure of Timosh, symbolising the hopes and eventual fulfilment of the Ukrainian people.

Timosh makes another appearance in *Arsenal*, an epic canvas covering Ukrainian history from the First World War to the Russian Civil War, as experienced in Kiev, and culminating in fighting around the arsenal in the heart of the city. In contrast to Eisenstein's fluid and dynamic camera movement, Dovzhenko essentially uses a static camera, but with much use of montage and cross-cutting: early in the film a woman beating a child is inter-cut with a man beating a horse. Elsewhere men and horses communicate, they speak to each other and hear each other. Where Dovzhenko is clearly distinctive, however, is his placing of human events against the majestic backdrop of nature, in particular the sky. Man and nature are one, as a dying Bolshevik asks his comrades to transport and bury him in his native soil.

In his pictures of life in the trenches during the First World War, Dovzhenko shows us crowds of soldiers, explosions, a torn landscape and stark silhouettes of soldiers against a vast sky. Massed ranks of faceless soldiers march to nowhere, laughing gas creates hideously incongruous pictures of smiling corpses, and disembodied hands protrude obscenely from the earth. A crazed German soldier is unable to stop himself from laughing, and we are unsure whether this is only from the effects of the gas, or whether he is descending into lunacy. History is being made on an epic scale, and the film features actual historical figures, such as Nicholas II, the Ukrainian nationalist leader Semen Petliura, and even a portrait of the national poet Taras Shevchenko which briefly comes to life.

Arsenal is notable for the sheer scale of its sets, creating a harrowing picture of war. Dovzhenko's quick cuts and montage of various images create a composite picture of the horror and madness of war, with some horrific images of faces twisted in death. Again, Dovzhenko impressively catches the right balance of the momentous and the personal, as his pictures of human misery are set against the grandeur and majesty of the sky. Dovzhenko also stages a train crash very impressively, as soldiers try to drive a train themselves, and spectacularly fail. The film is constructed as if a literary text, with certain motifs recurring throughout. At the beginning we see a grief-stricken mother who has lost three sons in the fighting. Towards the end we see a grieving mother, wife and daughter, as their menfolk are shot. This picture of sadness and loneliness is caught well by the director, and serves to give his picture of conflict a palpably human dimension.

Although *Arsenal* is obviously a pro-Bolshevik film, Dovzhenko's treatment of Ukrainian nationalism is ambivalent, to say the least. Much time is given to showing a political meeting where the nationalists are upstaged by the Bolshevik orators, but the camera lingers on the symbolism associated with the nationalists: the icons, priests processing in their finery, portraits of Taras Shevchenko, the nineteenth-century poet who is the symbol of Ukrainian culture and identity. Although the overall picture of the nationalists is negative, nevertheless it is also teasingly suggestive.

As the film reaches its climax with the fighting around the Kiev Arsenal, Dovzhenko again captures both the struggle of the masses as well as individual grief, when his camera wanders among large-scale battles and individual deaths. Throughout the film Dovzhenko fills the screen with close-ups of human faces, expressing the whole range of human emotions. Rows of corpses are juxtaposed with dozens of riderless horses, an image that recurs in *Earth* (and nearly forty years later in Alexander Askoldov's Civil War film *The Commissar* ('Komissar', 1967; released only in 1987).

The final image of the film is its most famous, as history enters the realms of mythology and legend. After three days of fighting and slaughter the nationalists are victorious. They begin executing all those who opposed them, and Timosh is about to be shot. He tears open his tunic and bares his chest, encouraging his executioners to fire. Bullets appear not to hit him, and his would-be executioners flee in panic. Dovzhenko therefore mythologises the inevitability of the workers' ultimate victory, and creates a vivid, unforgettable metaphor of the invincible proletarian mass, emerging victorious in their just cause.

Earth is regarded as Dovzhenko's masterpiece, the filmic equivalent of a lyrical poem, and deserves to have its celebrated niche in the history of world cinema. It is a tribute to man's bond with the land, and its opening shots place us firmly in the territory of the lyrical epic. The film begins in suitably grand style, with shots of rolling fields, the sky and then a woman, a symbol of the archetypal link of people and land, with close-ups of sunflowers, fruit and human faces all juxtaposed. Dovzhenko's film is also profoundly humanistic, as it concentrates on the death of the old man Semen in its early reels. Semen dies in peace, at one with the earth and the natural world, with a Tolstoian acceptance of the fact of death as a natural process. As he lies dying, Dovzhenko inter-cuts with a shot of a sunflower bent over and seemingly in mourning, and children eating apples, emphasising the fundamental unity of youth and old age, and man as an essential part of the natural process.

FIGURE 6 *Earth: the future beckons*

This ten-minute prologue then gives way to the main subject of the film: the struggle of villagers with kulaks, the rich peasants who were seen as the class enemy in the countryside. The kulaks are shown as grasping and selfish, opposed to new machinery and prepared to hide grain, kill their own livestock and even murder political activists. The arrival of machinery helps with the building of the new world. The political struggle is mirrored in the generational lack of mutual understanding between the peasant farmer Vasil and his father Panas. When Vasil is killed by kulaks, his father sees the light and joins the cause. What is unusual for European and American cinema, but a characteristic of Soviet cinema in these years, is the presentation on screen, through close-ups of grieving faces and inconsolable grief, of raw emotion, such as the heart-rending sadness of Vasil's father. Indeed, Dovzhenko shows a consistent predilection for hyperbole and grandeur.

Amid the turbulent world of human passions nature remains impassive and majestic. Dovzhenko delights in shots of the fields, with grass and sunflowers rustling in the wind as if they have a life of their own, and the vastness of the sky overhead. The director consistently shows us the natural unity of the world, man and animals, young and old. He is particularly fond of showing tiny human figures against the backdrop of a vast sky. The juxtaposition of scythes and tractors also encapsulates the bond being forged between the old and the new ways. Women joyously work in sun-drenched fields. Thus, there are many shots of the mechanised process of producing grain, where machinery symbolises the new world and the path to modernity. Man, nature and the machine are as one, as Dovzhenko shows in detail how the harvesting of wheat leads to the making of bread (it is very possible that Dovzhenko is poking fun here at Dziga Vertov, who in *Kino-Eye* had reversed the same process, showing how baked bread is returned to the fields).

As in *Arsenal*, Dovzhenko's camera is largely static, with long shots of people and landscape, as if the director is self-consciously painting an epic picture with grandiose images. As with Eisenstein's silent films, the Church is portrayed negatively. Panas turns away from the Church following his son's death. Vasil's funeral is not attended by any priests, but all the people from the village are there. The priest calls on God to strike down the unbelievers, an appeal for Judgement Day in the face of the rebellion of the masses. However, there is also ambivalence, for Vasil's death is, as the Party orator makes explicit, a martyrdom for the cause. The idea of self-sacrifice for the benefit of others is one which is central to Orthodoxy, and can be seen to be the central crux of Dovzhenko's film, despite the ostensible criticism of the Orthodox Church and its minions. The motif of martyrdom is crucial to Socialist Realist art, and also figures strongly in the politically committed films of the 1920s that have been discussed throughout this book.

Dovzhenko includes vividly poetic images in this film which have had a lasting influence on subsequent Soviet directors. The shot of riderless horses racing through the fields is one which Askoldov will use three decades later in *The Commissar*. As nature weeps for Vasil, apples and other fruit lying on the ground splashed by rain will feature in a similar shot in Andrei Tarkovsky's *Ivan's Childhood* ('Ivanovo detstvo') in 1962.

Dovzhenko's *Earth* is constructed and realised as a poetic celebration of man's unity with the natural world. Individuals admire the majesty and tranquillity of the moon-lit sky and fields, and stand in awe. Vasil dances in the moonlight just before he is shot, and his unhinged murderer dances wildly in the fields and village cemetery. The beginning of the film makes the lyrical theme explicit, and the film ends with a poetic symmetry. A peasant woman gives birth as Vasil is buried; as his coffin is carried through the fields on a cart the sunflowers waving in the wind seem to bow their heads in deference to the departed man. The published script makes the link of man and nature here explicit: 'When they carried him past the sunflowers, the fruits and the flowers almost touched his clear face giving him such an expression that there were many who couldn't restrain themselves from crying out in unbearable protest'.[1] The funeral, indeed, is filmed as a pagan ritual as the mourners sing and worship nature, and the Earth itself grieves.

The last few shots are of a couple gazing into each other's eyes lovingly, as they look forward to a radiant future. A Party orator announces that the class enemy is doomed, and the assembled masses look up to him as if to a deity. As he points to the sky to a 'Bolshevik aeroplane', the people look above him and to the heavens. The Party has taken the place of God. We see from the expressions on the kulaks' faces that they realise themselves that as a class they are now doomed. Dovzhenko succeeds in merging lyricism and ideology in a film that both celebrates the unity of creation and demonstrates that political progress is an organic part of the natural process. The British film theorist Paul Rotha (1931: 139) commented that:

Whilst the subject matter deals to a certain extent with the contemporary Soviet problem of the adoption of collective farming, as did *The General Line*, the real intent of *Earth* is the cinematic representation of nature and the expression of a new attitude towards birth, life and death, set in an environment of extreme natural beauty ... No better example of screen movement could be introduced than that of the gradually increasing tempo of the gathering of the harvest, the binding, the stacking, the sifting, the dough-kneading, and finally the baking of the bread, the movement so speeded up that at the finale the whole screen is rocking with energy.

Like Eisenstein, Dovzhenko shows history as being made by men. Women are almost absent in *Arsenal*, apart from as grieving family members, and in *Earth* they are symbols of motherhood and fertility. We can see that both Pudovkin and Kuleshov portray women as much more active and politically conscious. Dovzhenko retains a conservatism which will become more apparent in his increasingly orthodox later films. All the more pity, then, that Dovzhenko's subsequent films pay homage not to the unity of man and nature, but to the Communist Party and Stalin. *Shchors*, made in 1939, is a typical example of Socialist Realism under Stalin, with few redeeming artistic features. Based on the figure of the Civil War Red Army commander Alexander Shchors, it features clearly defined black-and-white characters, traditional Socialist Realist heroics, and a hero who is an embodiment of pure ideology. Notwithstanding this, the film offers a tantalising glimpse of the Dovzhenko of ten years previously. It opens with shots of fields of sunflowers, and partisans who seem to rise up from the earth itself to ambush and do battle with the occupying Germans. Explosions rock the landscape as the earth itself rebels against the foreign invader. These recollections of an earlier, more independent and creative Dovzhenko only serve to reinforce the sadness at his subsequent descent into conservative mediocrity.

Yet the film *Shchors* is perhaps more representative of the 'real' Dovzhenko than the films of the 1920s. The heroes of *Zvenigora*, *Arsenal*, and *Earth* all lead inexorably toward their logical successor, Shchors. Shchors himself is a man totally without human passions, he neither drinks nor smokes, and even when he thinks of his wife after defeating the Ukrainian nationalist leader Petliura, he merely dictates a telegram to her via an assistant. As he proudly boasts, 'The revolutionary goal always triumphs over personal interests.' He is that embodiment of revolutionary consciousness that is typical of the Socialist Realist positive hero. He does not speak or argue, he declaims. We know that he is the repository of truth because several times he reveals that 'Lenin told me'. He simply has to walk into a room for women to declare their undying devotion to him, and when he turns up at a village wedding, the prospective bride throws herself at him. From the very beginning we are never in doubt that he has heroic status.

Shchors belongs to that category of Soviet film, like the Vasilevs' *Chapaev* of 1934, where the hero is accorded mythical status in accordance with the Stalinist interpretation of historical progress. Indeed, Dovzhenko reveals that the whole idea of the film, right down to its themes and images, was Stalin's idea, in an article of 1937:

'Now I'll tell you why I summoned you,' Comrade Stalin said. 'When I spoke to you last time about *Shchors* I was giving you some advice. I was merely thinking of what you might do in the Ukraine. But neither my words nor newspaper articles put you under any obligation. You are a free man. If you want to make *Shchors*, do so – but, if you have other plans, do something else. Don't be embarrassed. I summoned you so that you should know this.'[2]

Of course no one, least of all those in the creative intelligentsia during the terror years of the 1930s, would ignore Stalin's 'advice'. Dovzhenko goes on to describe Stalin's ideas of how to make the film, ideas which, we can be sure, were tantamount to instructions:

Essentially I see a film about Shchors as a film about the uprising of the Ukrainian people, their victorious struggle with the Ukrainian counter-revolution and the German and Polish occupying forces for their social and national liberation,' Comrade Stalin said. In depicting Shchors and his heroic advisors, we must depict the Ukrainian people, the qualities of their national character, their humour and their beautiful songs and dances.[3]

So it was that the lyrical nationalism of Dovzhenko's cinema of the 1920s was turned by Stalin into a blunt instrument of Party propaganda. *Shchors* contains very little of the Dovzhenko of the previous decade, but does bear witness to his willingness to be subdued by the whim of the dictator. Solzhenitsyn's political prisoner X123 could equally direct his scorn at the Dovzhenko of the 1930s as at Eisenstein. Ukraine and its people are reduced to little more than bit players in the greater historical struggle. Ukrainians speak Russian with quaint accents, often used for comic effect, and the Red forces are greeted by happy, smiling Ukrainians with folk dances and singing, universal revelling to go with the traditional bread and salt offering. Ukrainians are represented as folksy yokels, who realise that their national interests lie with the Bolsheviks. As a film *Shchors* is deplorable, but as a document detailing Stalin's role in cultural affairs, and the subsequent ruination of a national talent, it is invaluable.

The career of Alexander Dovzhenko is remarkable in the history of Soviet cinema. He is undoubtedly a nationalist at heart, but finds himself increasingly harnessed to the political forces of the 1930s. Certainly, *Earth* is a marvellous poetic film, but subsequent films can be seen as little more than an attempt to curry favour with political bosses and ensure personal survival in an age when other artists were heading for the Gulag. His contribution to world cinema remains, however, in those masterpieces of the 1920s, especially *Arsenal* and *Earth*, where he mixes history, myth, and melodrama to create images which are both unforgettable and unique.

CONCLUSION: CULTURAL REVOLUTION AND THE END OF INNOVATION

Iakov Protazanov's 1928 comedy *Don Diego and Pelageia* concerns an illiterate peasant woman, Pelageia Demina, who is arrested, fined and imprisoned for the innocuous 'crime' of crossing the railway track at the wrong place. She is eventually released due to the efforts of her husband, and the young members of the *Komsomol*, but the real story of the film is the oppression of the peasant mass exercised by an uncaring, smug and self-serving bureaucracy. Although the film has a conventional happy ending, and was praised by critics for its exposé of the evils of bureaucratism, its very subject matter offers a telling picture of the relationship between the governors and the governed in the latter half of the 1920s. The Party was unequivocally in control, broached no dissent from those over whom it ruled, and abrogated to itself the sole right to dispense power and justice. Such was the reality of Soviet power, and film-makers were soon to find themselves similarly harangued and bullied by the ideologists.

Lev Kuleshov, Sergei Eisenstein, Vsevolod Pudovkin, Dziga Vertov and Alexander Dovzhenko were all supporters of the 'new world' ushered in by the Bolsheviks in 1917, although they may have been critical of certain aspects. They saw their duty as film-makers in promoting this new world, and none of them seriously questioned the Party's right to rule. It is therefore problematic to call their art truly 'revolutionary', for it did not seek to subvert existing pieties or question the official Marxist-Leninist vision of history. Indeed, they strove actively to serve the state. In terms of style, technique, artistic vision and in their theoretical contributions to film art, the likes of Eisenstein, Kuleshov, Vertov and Pudovkin were truly radical and remain to this day highly influential.

It is true to say that Soviet cinema was born in the fiery years of the Civil War, when film-makers were faced with great challenges and were forced to work in often arduous conditions. Because of the legacy of these directors, it is also true that without them the nature of world cinema would be very different today. With the benefit of hindsight, however, the contemporary observer must not forget that their art served to buttress a regime that came to power through force of arms and subsequently, and relentlessly, eliminated its opponents (the Tsar and his entire family, for instance, were among the first of millions of victims). The moral culpability of these directors, as well as many other Soviet writers, artists and musicians, in perpetuating a murderous regime should not be forgotten when trying to evaluate their overall contribution to the cultural consciousness of the modern world.

The 1920s were a remarkable decade in the history of Soviet culture, and there would never again be as much freedom granted to Soviet artists until the arrival of Mikhail Gorbachev as Communist Party General Secretary in 1985. The dominant theme in the 1920s was the new world of Lenin and Stalin, and the individual's place in it. Cinema, literature and art strove to describe and interpret this new world, and searched for diverse, innovative ways to depict it. Artists of the time were actively inspired by the desire to contribute to the new cultural environment, and even to the socio-political reality, fired by a genuine idealism.

Experiment and innovation were tolerated, indeed encouraged, by a Party machine that was still too concerned with political in-fighting. Stalin became Secretary of the Communist Party on Lenin's death in 1924, and finally succeeded in defeating his main rival Leon Trotsky in 1927, and exiling him in 1928. He then defeated the Right opposition in the Party in 1929. From the mid-1920s debates on industrialisation (the Five Year Plans, the first of which was introduced in 1929) and the proposed collectivisation of agriculture became subsumed in the policy of the 'socialist construction' of society. These were the topics that occupied the main areas of political discourse following Lenin's death.

When these questions were finally resolved to the satisfaction of Stalin at the end of the decade, the arts were required to contribute, but under much stricter guidance and direction from above. The new challenges to Soviet cinema in the period of 'Stalin's revolution' are summed up by the resolution of the Party Conference on Cinema in 1928:

The socio-political tasks of cinema in the USSR are the direct antithesis of those of bourgeois cinema. The whole ideological stance of Soviet cinema is different because the ideology of the proletariat must lie at the basis of the content of Soviet cinema. Cinema can and must be guided by the 'correct criteria of socio-political content' in its artistic production, criteria that are determined by the problems and the experience of construction by the proletariat in the spheres of economics, culture, the political organisation of the masses and of everyday life in the period of socialist construction.

Hence the socio-political content of Soviet cinema amounts to propaganda through the depiction of the new socialist elements in the economy, in social relations, in everyday life and in the personality of man; to struggle against the remnants of the old order; to the enlightenment of the masses, in their education and organisation around the cultural, economic and political tasks of the proletariat and its Party, realised in the period of socialist construction; to the class elucidation of historical events and social phenomena; to the dissemination of general knowledge and international education of the masses, to overcoming the nationalist prejudices and provincial narrow-mindedness of the masses and giving them access through cinema to the greatest achievements of world culture; to the organisation of leisure and entertainment, but in such a way that even 'entertainment' material in cinema organises the ideas and the feelings of the audience in the direction that the proletariat requires.[1]

It is to be noted that entertainment was the last of the Party's priorities, and it would be understood that any 'direction' would be defined by the Party itself. It was clear that cinema, as part of the political process, had to be controlled and directed by those who could ensure that it conveyed the Party's message.

A film culture that was based on montage and stylistic experiment was not one that could significantly help the mass mobilisation required to modernise the country. Critics of the 1920s were frustrated at the lukewarm response of the proletariat to such distinguished icons of the revolutionary struggle as *Battleship Potemkin*. Many workers simply did not understand it, were bored by it, and were just as uninterested in theoretical questions of montage and acting techniques. The Party may have wanted them to be educated, but the workers wanted to be entertained. The official requirement of a 'cinema for the millions', as Boris Shumiatsky, head of the Soviet film industry from 1930 until his execution as a 'saboteur' in 1938, put it in his book of 1935, was incompatible with the directorial autonomy of an Eisenstein, Vertov or Dovzhenko. Their stylistic virtuosity came under increasing attack in the 1930s as examples of 'formalism', the alleged preference for form over ideological content. Peter Kenez (1992: 103) remarks:

The cultural revolution in cinema was born out of frustration among politicians. The cinema did not live up to their expectations: directors wanted to please their audiences and produced romances and adventure stories with little ideological content. Great directors, like Eisenstein, Dovzhenko, Pudovkin, and Vertov, who were ideologically motivated and did produce films with 'correct' messages, also could not serve the purposes of the agitators, because the experimental style of the finest directors alienated the audiences. It was above all against these directors that the critics directed their fire. The charge against them was 'formalism' ... In the polemics against 'formalism' in cinema, however, the term came to describe any concern with the specifically aesthetic aspect of film-making, any deviation from a simple narrative line, and any artistic innovation.

It is indeed ironic that these directors, who had done more than anyone else to create a particularly 'Soviet' cinema, were precisely the ones singled out by critics in the 1930s. Any semblance of artistic autonomy thus came to an end in the early 1930s. In the film industry the role of the director became secondary to the importance of the script, a script that had to pass through several stages of an editing and consultation process (read: censorship) and, once approved, could not be changed without official authorisation. In the early 1930s this led to the 'script crisis', where fewer and fewer films were actually completed. In 1934 the first Soviet Writers' Congress articulated the method of socialist realism, and established it as the only possible means of artistic expression. What this in effect meant for all those active in the creative intelligentsia was that the Party no longer simply told them what they could not do – prohibiting anti-Soviet sentiments, for instance – it was now instructing them what they should do. Film, like literature, art and music, was required to become more accessible to the masses, as Maya Turovskaya (1993:96) makes clear:

The phenomenon of the Soviet cinema in the 1930s as 'the most mass-scale of the arts' did not originate in a vacuum but was preceded by more generalised processes. It rode on a sweeping shift in the cultural paradigm: from the avant-garde of the 'roaring twenties' toward a stabilising form of consciousness – in other words, toward narrative, 'accessible' structures in art in general. Also the industry was boosted by a technological coup: the advent and adaptation of sound that made this process particularly inevitable and pronounced in cinema.

In the 1930s Soviet cinema lost its last vestiges of directorial authority and stylistic innovation. The films of these years are aggressively propagan-distic, especially the political films of Kozintsev and Trauberg, and Mikhail Romm. Those that dealt with the countryside presented smiling, singing peasants who in reality were a universe away from the massively impoverished state of affairs that actually existed. Still, one of the favoured genres in the 1930s became the collective farm musical comedy, such as Grigory Alexandrov's *Volga-Volga* of 1938 or Ivan Pyrev's *Tractor Drivers* ('Traktoristy') a year later, films which ignored the calamitous cost of the collectivisation of agriculture and which painted a gloriously false but cheerfully upbeat picture of rural life. Above all, such films conformed to the dictates of socialist realism by offering a vision of life not as it was, but as it should be, and as it will be in the glorious future. By the end of the decade the showing of foreign films had just about stopped altogether. Soviet cinema audiences were treated to an exclusively Soviet product, one which repeated the platitudes of the political leadership and which divided the world conveniently into 'us' and 'them'.

It is nevertheless a tribute to the resilience and sheer imaginative genius of the Russian artist that, despite the restrictions of this and subsequent decades, great film-makers and great films emerged: Mikhail Romm, Mikhail Kalatozov, Andrei Tarkovsky, Vasily Shukshin all produced great films in the post-war years, and the 1960s saw the completion (but not the release) of perhaps the greatest film of the post-Stalin period, Alexander Askoldov's *The Commissar*. Made in 1967 but not shown until 1987, Askoldov's film was one of the last to be taken off the shelf to which Brezhnev's 'stagnation' had consigned it.

More than any other film of the Soviet period, *The Commissar* questions the values of devotion to the revolutionary cause and self-sacrifice as promoted by the likes of the Vasilevs' *Chapaev* (1934). Set during the Civil War, it includes motifs familiar from some of the classics of the 1920s, for instance riderless horses racing across a bullet-strewn landscape. It also features a key scene when a Bolshevik bares his chest to the hail of bullets coming at him from a White machine-gun. This replays the climactic scene in Dovzhenko's *Arsenal,* where Timosh bares his chest to the firing squad, who flee as the bullets appear not to hit home and the new order seems invincible. In Askoldov's film, however, the bullets do hit, and the erstwhile hero dies. Askoldov debunks the heroicisation of the Civil War, substitutes realism for the myth, and demonstrates, forty years on, that the idealism of the cinematic generation of the 1920s was misplaced.

Just as the 'golden age' of Soviet cinema was not born in a vacuum, so the talents of post-war – and now post-Soviet – directors developed from a rich and multi-textured soil. Lenin was said to have been convinced in 1922 that, for the Bolsheviks, film was the most important art form in propagating ideology, but time has since shown that it is also arguably Russian culture's most significant and abiding contribution to the twentieth century. The films and writings of Kuleshov, Eisenstein, Pudovkin, Vertov, and Dovzhenko, as well as others in the 1920s, are enduring landmarks in the development of Soviet film in a remarkable decade. Yet because we cannot separate art from politics in the Soviet Union, we must also not forget that these artists, innovative and daring as they were, supported and helped propagate the ideology of a regime that came to power by force, and which used violence against its citizens on a massive scale. The words of Solzhenitsyn's X123 remain relevant to all Soviet artists who aspired to greatness: just how far can we admire technical ability, even brilliance, without taking into account its contribution to the political oppression of the age? Time and psychological distance are still needed for an adequate and balanced consideration of this question.

NOTES

INTRODUCTION: THE GOLDEN AGE OF SOVIET CINEMA

1   One of the most informative accounts of the period is Sheila Fitzpatrick, *The Russian Revolution 1917–1932*. Oxford and New York: Oxford University Press, 1982. A full account of both the historical events and the cultural background of these years is available in Geoffrey Hosking, *A History of the Soviet Union*. London: Fontana Press, 1984.
2   The best and most detailed account of the cinema in pre-Revolutionary Russia (1896–1920) is Yuri Tsivian, *Early Cinema in Russia and its Cultural Reception*, trans. Alan Bodger, Chicago and London: University of Chicago Press, 1991.
3   See also the press reactions gathered in Iangirov (1998: 15–18).
4   One of the quirks of Soviet cinema is that the most popular foreign star of the 1920s was not Fairbanks or Pickford, but the now-forgotten German actor Harry Piel (1892–1963). Known as the 'German Douglas Fairbanks', Piel made his first film in 1912, both as actor and director, and went on to make over eighty films before 1930. His career declined with the coming of sound, and after the Second World War he largely directed shorts and documentaries. Siegfried Kracauer defines Piel's film persona: 'From the very beginning Piel seems to have been the type he was to impersonate in the future: that of a chivalrous dare-devil who excels in defeating resourceful criminals and rescuing innocent maidens ... His films were in the black and white style of the dime novels rather than the shadings of psychological conflicts; they superseded tragic issues with happy endings and, on the whole, presented a German variation of the Anglo-American thriller. This bright and pleasing trash stands isolated against a mass of sombre 'artistic' products.' See *From Caligari to Hitler: A Psychological History of the German Film*. Princeton: Princeton University Press, 1947: 25–6.
5   Quoted in Taylor and Christie (eds) 1994: 209–10.

CHAPTER ONE: LEV KULESHOV: THE ORIGINS OF MONTAGE IN SOVIET CINEMA

1   Quoted in Taylor and Christie (eds) 1994: 46.

2 The Church of Christ the Saviour (Khram Khrista Spasitelia) was demolished in 1931 to make way for a huge open air swimming pool, as part of a plan for the redevelopment of Moscow. The pool existed until 1993. Wits in the Soviet Union would say that it was a most fitting place to have a swimming pool, as the city's atheistic population could bathe in holy water. The pool was removed in 1993, and from 1995 the restoration of the church took place. The new Church of Christ the Saviour was officially opened in 1997, during the celebrations for the 850th anniversary of the founding of Moscow.

CHAPTER TWO: SERGEI EISENSTEIN: THE MYTHO-POETICS OF REVOLUTION

1 Similarly, Jay Leyda discusses the sheer power of *Battleship Potemkin*, which was so great that participants in the actual mutiny twenty years previously believed that what they were seeing on the screen was a true reflection of fact: 'Eisenstein once received a letter from one of the mutineers, thanking him for the film, and identifying himself as 'one of those under the tarpaulin'. Eisenstein did not have the heart to tell him that the tarpaulin had been a dramatic invention – but he was interested in how even an eye-witness, a participant, after exposure to the power of empathy, could revise his memory of the fact.' See *Kino: A History of the Russian and Soviet Film* (2nd edn.). London: 1973: 199.

2 Quoted in Taylor 1998: 138.

CHAPTER THREE: VSEVOLOD PUDOVKIN: CONFLICT AND STRUGGLE AS FILM ART

1 The anti-cosmopolitan campaign was an officially inspired anti-Semitic campaign of the late 1940s, intended to root out what were euphemistically referred to as 'rootless cosmopolitans'. These were Jews in prominent positions, who allegedly held no loyalty toward the Soviet State. The campaign coincided with the establishment of the state of Israel.

2 *Chess Fever* was co-directed by Nikolai Shpikovsky. Denise Youngblood believes he actually did most of the work on it, rather than Pudovkin. See *Movies for the Masses: Popular Cinema and Soviet Society in the 1920s*. Cambridge and New York: Cambridge University Press, 1992: 216.

3 Temple Willcox quotes official British documents from the time that record the alarm felt in some circles that these scenes may provoke revolt in parts of the British Empire, in particular India. See 'Soviet Films, Censorship and the British Government: A Matter of the Public Interest', in *Historical Journal of Film, Radio and Television*, 10, 3, 1990: 275–92.

CHAPTER FOUR: DZIGA VERTOV: LIFE 'CAUGHT UNAWARES'

1 Quoted in Taylor and Christie (eds) 1994: 69.

2 Quoted in Tamara Selezneva, *Kinomysl 1920-kh godov*. Leningrad: Iskusstvo, 1972: 31.

3 Quoted in Taylor and Christie (eds) 1994: 94. Subsequently Vertov was to complain that other directors of fictional films were stealing his ideas (in particular Eisenstein, in his shots of crowds of workers in *Strike* and *Battleship Potemkin*).

4   Quoted in Anna Lawton (ed.), *The Red Screen: Politics, Society, Art in Soviet Cinema*. New York: Routledge, 1992: 107–8.

5   Quoted in Bowlt and Matich (eds), *Laboratory of Dreams: The Russian Avant-Garde and Cultural Experiment*. Stanford: Stanford University Press, 1996: 217.

6   Quoted in Ali Issari and Paul, *What is Cinéma Vérité?* Metuchen, New Jersey and London: The Scarecrow Press, 1979: 31.

CHAPTER FIVE: ALEXANDER DOVZHENKO: UKRAINIAN NATIONALIST CINEMA

1   See *Two Russian Film Classics: Mother (Pudovkin); Earth (Dovzhenko)* London: Lorrimer Publishing, 1973: 100.

2   Quoted in Taylor and Christie (eds) 1994: 384.

3   Ibid.

CONCLUSION: CULTURAL REVOLUTION AND THE END OF INNOVATION

1   Quoted in Taylor and Christie (eds) 1994: 128–9.

FILMOGRAPHY

Admiral Nakhimov ('Admiral Nakhimov') (Vsevolod Pudovkin, 1947, USSR)

Adventures of Oktiabrina, The ('Pokhozhdeniia Oktiabriny') (Grigory Kozintsev and Leonid Trauberg, 1924, USSR)

Aelita ('Aelita') (Iakov Protazanov, 1924, USSR)

Aerograd ('Aerograd') (Alexander Dovzhenko, 1935, USSR)

Alexander Nevsky ('Aleksandr Nevsky') (Sergei Eisenstein, 1938, USSR)

Arsenal ('Arsenal') (Alexander Dovzhenko, 1929, USSR)

Baby Doll (Elia Kazan, 1956, US)

Battleship Potemkin ('Bronenosets Potemkin') (Sergei Eisenstein, 1926, USSR)

Bear's Wedding, The ('Medvezhia svadba') (Anatoly Lunacharsky, 1925, USSR)

Bed and Sofa ('Tretia Meshchanskaia') (Abram Room, 1927, USSR)

Bezhin Meadow ('Bezhin lug') (Sergei Eisenstein, 1936-38, USSR)

Birth of a Nation, The (D. W. Griffith, 1915, US)

Borderlands ('Okraina') (Boris Barnet, 1933, USSR)

By the Law ('Po zakonu') (Lev Kuleshov, 1926, USSR)

Case of the Three Million, The ('Protsess o trekh millionakh') (Iakov Protazanov, 1926, USSR)

Chapaev ('Chapaev') (Vasilev Brothers, 1934, USSR)

Chess Fever ('Shakhmatnaia goriachka') (Vsevolod Pudovkin, 1925, USSR)

Commissar, The ('Komissar') (Alexander Askoldov, 1967, USSR)

Death Ray, The ('Luch smerti') (Lev Kuleshov, 1925, USSR)

Departure of the Great Old Man ('Ukhod velikogo startsa') (Iakov Protazanov, 1911, Russia)

Devil's Wheel, The ('Chertovo koleso') (Grigory Kozintsev and Leonid Trauberg, 1926, USSR)

Deserter, The ('Dezertir') (Vsevolod Pudovkin, 1933, USSR)

Don Diego and Pelageia ('Don Diego i Pelageia') (Iakov Protazanov, 1928, USSR)

Don Quixote ('Don Kikhot') (Grigory Kozintsev, 1958, USSR)

Dr Mabuse the Gambler (Fritz Lang, 1922, Ger.)

Earth ('Zemlia') (Alexander Dovzhenko, 1930, USSR)

Eleventh Year, The ('Odinnadtsatyi') (Dziga Vertov, 1928, USSR)

Elusive Avengers, The ('Neulovimye mstiteli') (Edmond Keosaian, 1966, USSR)

End of St Petersburg, The ('Konets Sankt-Peterburga') (Vsevolod Pudovkin, 1927, USSR)

Engineer Prite's Project ('Proekt Inzhenera Praita') (Lev Kuleshov, 1918, RSFSR)

Enthusiasm ('Entuziazm') (Dziga Vertov, 1931, USSR)

Extraordinary Adventures of Mr West in the Land of the Bolsheviks, The ('Neobychainye prikliucheniia mistera Vesta v strane bolshevikov') (Lev Kuleshov, 1924, USSR)

Fall of the Romanov Dynasty, The ('Padenie dinastii Romanovykh') (Esfir Shub, 1927, USSR)

Fantômas (Louis Feuillade, 1913–14, Fr.)

Father Sergius ('Otets Sergii') (Iakov Protazanov, 1918, RSFSR)

Festival of St Jorgen, The ('Prazdnik sviatogo Iorgena') (Iakov Protazanov, 1930, USSR)

Fitter and the Chancellor, The ('Slesar i kantsler') (Vsevolod Pudovkin, 1924, USSR)

Forty-First, The ('Sorok pervyi') (Iakov Protazanov, 1927, USSR)

Fragment of Empire ('Oblomok imperii') (Fridrikh Ermler, 1929, USSR)

Gay Canary, The ('Veselaia kanareika') (Lev Kuleshov, 1929, USSR)

General Line, The ('Generalnaia linya') aka *The Old and the New* ('Staroe i novoe') (Sergei Eisenstein, 1929, USSR)

Girl with the Hatbox, The ('Devushka s korobkoi') (Boris Barnet, 1927, USSR)

Glumov's Diary ('Dnevnik Glumova') (Sergei Eisenstein, 1923, USSR)

Gold Rush, The (Charles Chaplin, 1925, US)

Great Citizen, The ('Velikii grazhdanin') (Fridrikh Ermler, 1938–39, USSR)

Great Consoler, The ('Velikii uteshitel') (Lev Kuleshov, 1933, USSR)

Great Path, The ('Velikii put') (Esfir Shub, 1927, USSR)

Greed (Erich von Stroheim, 1923, US)

Hammer and Sickle ('Serp i molot') (Vladimir Gardin, 1921, RSFSR)

Hamlet ('Gamlet') (Grigory Kozintsev, 1964, USSR)

Heir of Genghiz Khan, The ('Potomok Chingiz-Khana') (Vsevolod Pudovkin, 1928, USSR)

His Call ('Ego prizyv') (Iakov Protazanov, 1925, USSR)

House in the Snowdrifts, The ('Dom v sugrobakh') (Fridrikh Ermler, 1928, USSR)

House on Trubnaia Square, The ('Dom na Trubnoi') (Boris Barnet, 1928, USSR)

Hunger, Hunger, Hunger ('Golod, golod, golod') (Vladimir Gardin and Vsevolod Pudovkin, 1921, RSFSR)

Intolerance (D. W. Griffith, 1916, US)

Ivan ('Ivan') (Alexander Dovzhenko, 1932, USSR)

Ivan's Childhood ('Ivanovo detstvo') (Andrei Tarkovsky, 1962, USSR)

Ivan the Terrible, Part I ('Ivan Groznyi') (Sergei Eisenstein, 1942, USSR)

Ivan the Terrible, Part II ('Ivan Groznyi') (Sergei Eisenstein, 1946, USSR)

Katka the Apple Seller ('Katka – Bumazhnyi Ranet') (Fridrikh Ermler, 1926, USSR)

King Lear ('Korol Lir') (Grigory Kozintsev, 1971, USSR)

Kino-Eye ('Kino-glaz') (Dziga Vertov, 1924, USSR)

Kiss of Mary Pickford, The ('Potselui Meri Pikford') (Sergei Komarov, 1927, USSR)

Les Misérables (A. Capellani, 1913, Fr.)

Lev Tolstoy and the Russia of Nicholas II ('Lev Tolstoi i Rossiia Nikolaia II') (Esfir Shub, 1928, USSR)

Little Red Devils ('Krasnye diavoliata') (Ivan Perestiani, 1923, USSR)

Love's Little Berries ('Iagodki liubvi') (Alexander Dovzhenko, 1926, USSR)

Lullaby ('Kolybelnaia') (Dziga Vertov, 1937, USSR)

Man from the Restaurant, The ('Chelovek iz restorana') (Iakov Protazanov, 1927, USSR)

Man with the Movie Camera, The ('Chelovek s kinoapparatom') (Dziga Vertov, 1929, USSR)

Mark of Zorro, The (Rouben Mamoulian, 1940, US)

Maxim's Return ('Vozvrashchenie Maksima') (Grigory Kozintsev and Leonid Trauberg, 1937, USSR)

Maxim's Youth ('Iunost Maksima') (Grigory Kozintsev and Leonid Trauberg, 1934, USSR)

Mechanics of the Brain, The ('Mekhanika golovnogo mozga') (Vsevolod Pudovkin, 1925, USSR)

Ménage-à-trois ('Liubov vtroem') (Petr Todorovsky, 1998, Rus.)

Michurin ('Michurin') (Alexander Dovzhenko, 1949, USSR)

Minin and Pozharsky ('Minin i Pozharsky') (Vsevolod Pudovkin, 1939, USSR)

Miss Mend ('Miss Mend') (Boris Barnet, 1926, USSR)

Mother ('Mat') (Vsevolod Pudovkin, 1926, USSR)

New Babylon ('Novyi Vavilon') (Grigory Kozintsev and Leonid Trauberg, 1929, USSR)

Nosferatu (F. W. Murnau, 1922, Ger.)

October ('Oktiabr') (Sergei Eisenstein, 1927, USSR)

On the Red Front ('Na krasnom fronte') (Lev Kuleshov, 1920, RSFSR)

On the Waterfront (Elia Kazan, 1954, US)

Overcoat, The ('Shinel') (Grigory Kozintsev and Leonid Trauberg, 1926, USSR)

Parisian Cobbler, The ('Parizhskii sapozhnik') (Fridrikh Ermler, 1928, USSR)

Peasants ('Krestiane') (Fridrikh Ermler, 1934, USSR)

Poison ('Iad') (Anatoly Lunacharsky, 1927, USSR)

Prostitute, The ('Prostitutka') (Esfir Shub, 1926, USSR)

Queen of Spades, The ('Pikovaia dama') (Iakov Protazanov, 1916, Russia)

Ranks and People (Chiny i liudi) (Iakov Protazanov, 1929, USSR)

Return of Vasily Bortnikov ('Vozrashchenie Vasiliia Bortnikova') (Vsevolod Pudovkin, 1953, USSR)

Robin Hood (Allan Dwan, 1921, US)

Shchors ('Shchors') (Alexander Dovzhenko, 1939, USSR)

Simple Case, A ('Prostoi sluchai') (Vsevolod Pudovkin, 1932, USSR)

Sixth Part of the World, The ('Shestaia chast mira') (Dziga Vertov, 1926, USSR)

Stenka Razin ('Stenka Razin') (V. Romashkov, 1908, Russia)

Storm over Asia; aka *The Heir of Genghis Khan* ('Potomok Chingiz-Khana') (Vsevolod Pudovkin, 1928, USSR)

Stride, Soviet! ('Shagai, sovet!') (Dziga Vertov, 1926, USSR)

Strike ('Stachka') (Sergei Eisenstein, 1925, USSR)

Suram Fortress ('Suramskaia krepost') (Ivan Perestiani, 1923, USSR)

Suvorov ('Suvorov') (Vsevolod Pudovkin, 1941, USSR)

S.V.D.: The Union of the Great Cause ('S.V.D.: Soiuz Velikogo Dela') (Grigory Kozintsev and Leonid Trauberg, 1927, USSR)

Tailor from Torzhok, The ('Zakroishchik iz Torzhka') (Iakov Protazanov, 1925, USSR)

Thief of Baghdad, The (Michael Powell, 1940, UK)

Three Heroines ('Tri geroini') (Dziga Vertov, 1941, USSR)

Three Songs about Lenin ('Tri pesni o Lenine') (Dziga Vertov, 1934, USSR)

Thunder over Mexico (Sol Lesser, 1934, US)

Tractor Drivers ('Traktoristy') (Ivan Pyrev, 1939, USSR)

Twelve Angry Men (Sidney Lumet, 1957, US)

Unsung Song of Love, The ('Pesn liubvi nedopetaia') (Lev Kuleshov, 1919, RSFSR)

Untouchables, The (Brian De Palma, 1987, US)

Victory ('Pobeda') (Vsevolod Pudovkin, 1938, USSR)

Volga-Volga ('Volga-Volga') (Grigory Alexandrov, 1938, USSR)

Vyborg Side, The ('Vyborgskaia storona') (Grigory Kozintsev and Leonid Trauberg, 1939)

White Eagle, The ('Belyi orel') (Iakov Protazanov, 1928, USSR)

Young Lady and the Hooligan, The ('Baryshnia i khuligan') (E. Slavinsky, 1918, RSFSR)

Your Lady Friend ('Vasha znakomaia') (Lev Kuleshov, 1927, USSR)

Zhukovsky ('Zhukovsky') (Vsevolod Pudovkin, 1950, USSR)

Zvenigora ('Zvenigora') (Alexander Dovzhenko, 1928, USSR)

BIBLIOGRAPHY

The bibliography lists works cited in the text and is also designed to point to useful further reading. The annotated list of 'essential reading' highlights works considered to be of particular importance to contemporary understandings of Soviet cinema in its golden age, although many valuable contributions are also to be found under 'secondary reading'.

ESSENTIAL READING

Kenez, Peter (1992) *Cinema and Soviet Society, 1917–1953*. Cambridge and New York: Cambridge University Press.
    A clear and concise overview of Soviet cinema to the death of Stalin, with useful analysis of key films and directors. Very strong on the silent period.
Leyda, Jay (1973) *Kino: A History of the Russian and Soviet Film* (2nd edn.). London: George Allen and Unwin.
    Classic account first published in 1960, with personal insights and views on films and directors, especially in the 1920s and 1930s.
Taylor, Richard (1979) *The Politics of the Soviet Cinema, 1917–1929*. Cambridge and New York: Cambridge University Press.
    Extremely useful and readable analysis of the relationship of politics and cinema in the 1920s.
Taylor, Richard and Ian Christie (eds) (1991) *Inside the Film Factory: New Approaches to Russian and Soviet Cinema*. London and New York: Routledge.
    A major collection of articles mainly devoted to the 1920s, with contributions on Barnet and Protazanov, among others.
—— (1994) *The Film Factory: Russian and Soviet Cinema in Documents 1896–1939* (2nd edn.). London and New York: Routledge.
    An invaluable source of factual documentation.
Youngblood, Denise J. (1992) *Movies for the Masses: Popular Cinema and Soviet Society in the 1920s*. Cambridge and New York: Cambridge University Press.

Seminal account of early Soviet cinema, with much factual information and informed discussion of the cinema industry.

SECONDARY READING

Ali Issari, M. and Paul, Doris A. (1979) *What is Cinéma Vérité?* Metuchen, New Jersey and London: The Scarecrow Press.

Bergan, Ronald (1997) *Eisenstein: A Life in Conflict*. London: Little, Brown.

Bordwell, David (1993) *The Cinema of Eisenstein*. London and Cambridge, Massachusetts: Harvard University Press.

Bowlt, John E. and Olga Matich (eds) (1996) *Laboratory of Dreams: The Russian Avant-Garde and Cultural Experiment*. Stanford: Stanford University Press.

Clark, Katerina (1981) *The Soviet Novel: History as Ritual*. Chicago and London: University of Chicago Press.

Fitzpatrick, Sheila (1982) *The Russian Revolution 1917–1932*. Oxford and New York: Oxford University Press.

Graffy, Julian (1998) 'Cinema', in Kelly and Shepherd (eds), *Russian Cultural Studies: An Introduction*. Oxford and New York: Oxford University Press, 165–91.

Horton, Andrew and Michael Brashinsky (1992) *The Zero Hour: Glasnost and Soviet Cinema in Transition*. Princeton: Princeton University Press.

Hosking, Geoffrey (1984) *A History of the Soviet Union*. London: Fontana Press.

Iangirov, R. (1998) '*Tretia Meshchanskaia*: otkliki pressy', *Iskusstvo kino*, 1998, 3, 15–18.

Iurenev, Rostislav (1964) *Sovetskaia kinokomediia*. Moscow: Nauka.

Kelly, Catriona and David Shepherd (eds) (1998) *Russian Cultural Studies: An Introduction*. Oxford and New York: Oxford University Press.

Kepley, Vance, Jr. (1986) *In the Service of the State: The Cinema of Alexander Dovzhenko*. Madison: University of Wisconsin Press.

—— (1992) 'Mr Kuleshov in the Land of the Modernists', in Lawton (ed.), *The Red Screen: Politics, Society, Art in Soviet Cinema*. New York: Routledge, 132–47.

Khokhlova, E. S. (1999) 'Lev Kuleshov – 100. Iz naslediia rezhissera i pedagoga', in *Kinovedcheskie zapiski*, 41, 7–29.

Kracauer, Siegfried (1947) *From Caligari to Hitler: A Psychological History of the German Film*. Princeton: Princeton University Press.

Lahusen, Thomas and Gene Kuperman (eds) (1993) *Late Soviet Culture: From Perestroika to Novostroika*. Durham and London: Duke University Press.

Lawton, Anna (ed.) (1992) *The Red Screen: Politics, Society, Art in Soviet Cinema*. New York: Routledge.

Marshall, Herbert (1983) *Masters of the Soviet Cinema: Crippled Creative Biographies*. London: Routledge and Kegan Paul.

Mayne, Judith (1989) *Kino and the Woman Question*. Columbus: Ohio State University Press.

Petric, Vlada (1987) *Constructivism in Film: 'The Man with the Movie Camera'. A Cinematic Analysis*. Cambridge: Cambridge University Press.

—— (1992) 'Cinematic Abstraction as a Means of Conveying Ideological Messages in *The Man with the Movie Camera*', in Lawton (ed.), 90–112.

—— (1995) 'Vertov, Lenin and Perestroika: the Cinematic Transposition of Reality', in *Historical Journal of Film, Radio and Television*, 15, 1, 3–17.

Rotha, Paul (1931) *Celluloid: The Film Today*. London and New York: Longmans, Green and Co., 135–53.

Sadoul, Georges (1963) 'Bio-Filmographie de Dziga Vertov', in *Cahiers du Cinma*, 146, 21–9.

Selezneva, Tamara (1972) *Kinomysl 1920-kh godov*. Leningrad: Iskusstvo.

Seton, Marie (1978) *Sergei M. Eisenstein: A Biography* (2nd edn.). London: Dennis Dobson.

Solzhenitsyn, Alexander (1963) *One Day in the Life of Ivan Denisovich*, trans. Ralph Parker. Harmondsworth: Penguin.

Street, Sarah (1997) *British National Cinema*. London and New York: Routledge.

Taylor, Richard (ed. and trans.) (1988) *S. M. Eisenstein. Selected Works: Volume One. Writings 1922–34*. London: British Film Institute.

—— (1991) (trans. M. Glenny) *S. M. Eisenstein. Selected Works: Volume Two. Towards a Theory of Montage*. London: British Film Institute.

—— (1994) (trans. W. Powell) *S. M. Eisenstein. Selected Works: Volume Three. Beyond the Stars. The Memoirs of Sergei Eisenstein*. London: British Film Institute.

—— (1996) (trans. W. Powell) *S. M. Eisenstein. Selected Works: Volume Four. Writings 1934–47*. London: British Film Institute.

—— (ed.) (1998) *The Eisenstein Reader*. London: British Film Institute.

Taylor, Richard and Ian Christie (eds) (1993) *Eisenstein Rediscovered*. London and New York: Routledge.

Tsivian, Yuri (1991) *Early Cinema in Russia and its Cultural Reception*, trans. Alan Bodger, Chicago and London: University of Chicago Press.

Turovskaya, Maya (1993) 'The Tastes of Soviet Moviegoers in the 1930s' in Lahusen and Kuperman (eds), 95–107.

Usai, Paolo Cherchi, Yuri Tsivian, Lorenzo Codelli, Carlo Montanaro and David Robinson (eds) (1989) *Silent Witnesses: Russian Films 1908–1919*. London: British Film Institute.

Willcox, Temple (1990) 'Soviet Films, Censorship and the British Government: A Matter of the Public Interest', in *Historical Journal of Film, Radio and Television*, 10, 3, 275–92.

Yampolsky, Mikhail (1991) 'Kuleshov's Experiments and the New Anthropology of the Actor', in Taylor and Christie (eds), 31–50.

Zapasnik, T. E. and A. Petrovich (eds) (1989) *Pudovkin v vospominaniakh sovremennikov*. Moscow: Iskusstvo.

Zholkovsky, Alexander (1996) 'Eisenstein's Poetics: Dialogical or Totalitarian?', in Bowlt and Matich (eds), 245–56.

Zorkaya, Neya (1989) *The Illustrated History of the Soviet Cinema*. New York: Hippocrene Books.

INDEX OF NAMES